ONE DAY IN THE LIFE
OF IVAN DENISOVICH

D0143673

A Critical Companion

ONE DAY IN THE LIFE

OF IVAN DENISOVICH

A Critical Companion

Edited by Alexis Klimoff

Northwestern University Press

The American Association of Teachers

of Slavic and East European Languages

Northwestern University Press

Evanston, Illinois 60208-4210

Copyright © 1997 by Northwestern University Press

All rights reserved

Printed in the United States of America

Library of Congress Cataloging-in-Publication Data

One day in the life of Ivan Denisovich : a critical companion / edited

by Alexis Klimoff.

     p.   cm. — (Northwestern/AATSEEL critical companions to

Russian literature)

    Includes bibliographical references.

    ISBN 0-8101-1214-0 (paper : alk. paper)

    1. Solzhenitsyn, Aleksandr Isaevich, 1918– Odin den' Ivana

Denisovicha. I. Klimoff, Alexis. II. Series.

    PG3488.O40366 1997

891.73'44—dc21   97-21430

                                              CIP

ISBN 0-8101-1214-0

The paper used in this publication meets the minimum

requirements of the American National Standard for

Information Sciences — Permanence of Paper for Printed

Library Materials, ansi z39.48–1984.

Contents

Acknowledgments

Some of the material in this volume has been previously published in somewhat different form and appears here by permission: Selections from Aleksandr Solzhenitsyn, *The Oak and the Calf: Sketches of Literary Life in the Soviet Union*, translated by H. T. Willetts (New York: Harper and Row, 1980). Copyright © 1975 by Aleksandr I. Solzhenitsyn. English translation copyright © 1979, 1980 by Harper & Row, Publishers, Inc. Reprinted by permission of HarperCollins Publishers, Inc. Selections from Solzhenitsyn's supplement to this work, *Invisible Allies*, translated by Alexis Klimoff and Michael Nicholson (Washington, D.C.: Counterpoint, 1995). Copyright © 1992 by Aleksandr I. Solzhenitsyn. English translation copyright © 1995 by Aleksandr I. Solzhenitsyn. Reprinted by permission of the author and Counterpoint Press. Selections from Vladimir Lakshin, *"Novyi mir" vo vremena Khrushcheva: Dnevnik i poputnoe (1953–1964)* (Moscow: Knizhnaia palata, 1991). Copyright © 1991 by Vladimir Lakshin. Translated by Rebecca Park. Reprinted by permission of Svetlana N. Lakshina. Kornei Chukovskii, "Literaturnoe chudo," from the commentary section of Lidiia Chukovskaia, *Zapiski ob Anne Akhmatovoi*, vol. 2 (Paris: YMCA Press, 1980), pp. 608–9. Copyright © 1980 by YMCA Press. Translated by the editor. Reprinted by permission of YMCA Press. Mikhail Lifshitz, "O povesti A. I. Solzhenitsyna 'Odin den' Ivana Denisovicha'," *Voprosy literatury*, 1990, no. 7 (July), pp. 74–75. Copyright © 1990 by Voprosy literatury. Translated by the editor. Reprinted by permission of Voprosy literatury.

NOTE ON TRANSLITERATION

Russian words, names, and phrases are transcribed according to the Library of Congress system of transliteration in the case of all bibliographical references and linguistic citations. In most other contexts, a less formal system is in place: the traditional spelling of names like Tolstoy and Tvardovsky is retained, and frequently encountered names and titles relevant to *One Day* and its publication history are given as they are spelled in the texts cited, for example, Buynovsky, Alyoshka, *Novy Mir*, and so on.

I      INTRODUCTION

The Sober Eye: Ivan Denisovich and the Peasant Perspective

ALEXIS KLIMOFF

Let it be stated right at the start: the appearance of Aleksandr Solzhenitsyn's *One Day in the Life of Ivan Denisovich* in a Moscow journal in 1962 was an event that cannot be measured by literary standards alone. The publication became an instant political sensation, one greatly intensified by the knowledge that the work had received the personal imprimatur of Nikita Khrushchev, the head of the Soviet Communist Party at the time. The story of the unique confluence of circumstances that made this possible is set forth in the section of the present book entitled "The Road to Publication." Yet these political ramifications must not be allowed to obscure the achievement of *One Day* as a compelling work of literary art closely linked with the traditions of nineteenth-century Russian literature. The remarks that follow are largely devoted to these aspects of Solzhenitsyn's text.

Solzhenitsyn has told us a fair amount about the external circumstances in which *One Day in the Life of Ivan Denisovich* was conceived. From the annotation to the text of *One Day* as published in the Russian-language *Sobranie sochinenii* (Collected Works), we learn that the idea of writing a work of this type first came to the author in the winter of 1950–51, a time when he was a "general duty" forced laborer in a Soviet prison camp in Kazakhstan.[1] In a 1982 interview with the BBC timed to coincide with the twentieth anniversary of the publication of *One Day*, Solzhenitsyn elaborated on this particular moment:

On one long winter workday in camp, as I was lugging a handbarrow [filled with mortar] together with another man, I asked myself how one might portray the totality of our camp existence. In essence it should suffice to give a thorough description of a single day, providing minute detail and focusing on the most ordinary kind of worker: that would reflect our entire experience. It wouldn't even be necessary to give examples of any particular horrors. It shouldn't be an extraordinary day at all, but rather a completely unremarkable one, the kind of day that will add up to years. That was my conception, and it lay dormant in my mind for nine years.[2]

The nine years to which Solzhenitsyn refers were filled with momentous changes in his life. This included his release from prison camp (1953), his recovery from a near-fatal bout with cancer (1954), the move to European Russia after three years of compulsory residence in a tiny Central Asian hamlet (1956), and his legal "rehabilitation" (1957), that is, the formal annulment of the charges that had led to his arrest for criticizing Stalin back in 1945.

In the spring of 1958, when Solzhenitsyn was teaching physics and astronomy in a Ryazan secondary school, but devoting every scrap of free time to his clandestine writing (he was then working on the novel *The First Circle*), he began to give serious thought to producing a history of the Soviet system of prisons and labor camps. He sketched out a preliminary outline of what would later become *The Gulag Archipelago*, actually writing drafts of a number of chapters, but concluded that this undertaking had to be set aside as overambitious for the amount of data at his disposal.[3] The point to note here is that even though this particular project remained unfinished at the time, it was already the fourth of Solzhenitsyn's works focused on the Soviet machinery of repression. As a result, *One Day in the Life of Ivan Denisovich*, which was written in the following year, needs to be recognized as part of a developing series.[4]

The final impulse for the creation of *One Day* seems to have been provided by Solzhenitsyn's attempt, in the spring of 1959, to portray the life of a schoolteacher by describing one day on the job.[5] This venture does not seem to have come to fruition, however, and in its stead Solzhenitsyn launched into the work with the similarly limited time frame that he had conceived in camp many years earlier. As he phrased it in the BBC interview quoted above, "Only in 1959, nine years later, did I sit down and write it."[6] And, as he added on another occasion, "I sat down, and the story simply gushed out with tremendous force! That's because there were so many of these days all penned up inside me. And it was simply a question of making sure that nothing would be left out."[7]

Work proceeded quickly, taking up only some forty days in total.[8] The original title chosen by Solzhenitsyn was *Shch-854 (Odin den' odnogo zeka)* (Shch-854 [One Day in the Life of a Zek]), the first part referring to the protagonist's prison identification number and the word *zek* derived from *z/k*, the Soviet-era abbreviation for an inmate of prisons or forced-labor camps. The writer has said the following about the central character depicted in his work: "The figure of Ivan Denisovich [Shukhov] combines the traits of the soldier Shukhov, a man who had been the author's comrade-in-arms during the war against Germany (and who had never been in prison), with the common experience of camp inmates as well as with the author's own experiences as a bricklayer in a Special Camp."[9]

The Shukhov of biographical reality had served in the sound-ranging artillery battery under Solzhenitsyn's command, but the writer has stated that he had not been on any particularly friendly terms with this simple soldier.[10] It is therefore all the more interesting to hear Solzhenitsyn's account of the mysterious creative process whereby certain traits of a man he had known only casually came to be transposed onto the main protagonist of *One Day*:

When I had hit upon the idea of describing a day in the life of a zek, it was of course clear that he would have to be the most ordinary of rank-and-file members in the Gulag army. . . . The question was whom I should pick. I had rubbed shoulders with numerous prisoners in my time and could remember dozens and dozens of individuals I had known well, even hundreds. Then suddenly and for no apparent reason, the figure of Ivan Denisovich began to take shape in a most unexpected fashion. First the surname – Shukhov – forced itself upon me without any conscious choice on my part; this was the family name of a soldier in my battery during the war. Then, along with his surname, came his face and a few aspects of his biography: the region he was from, the way he spoke. And so this private from an artillery unit serving in the German-Soviet war began to enter into my tale, even though he had never done time in prison. . . . It was as if he had clambered in of his own accord.[11]

This figure then acquired additional biographical details and personality traits drawn from a number of Solzhenitsyn's fellow prisoners, as well as reflecting some of the writer's own views and feelings. The other characters portrayed in *One Day* are less "composite" in nature and tend to be more consistently linked to particular individuals. And all of them, Solzhenitsyn tells us, "are taken from the experience of camp, and endowed with actual biographies."[12] And in fact we do know from a variety of sources that Captain Buynovsky was largely based on Solzhenitsyn's campmate Boris Burkovsky; that Tyurin, the tough foreman of Shukhov's work gang, reflected the experiences of a man partially identified by Solzhenitsyn (in *The Gulag Archipelago*) as Nikolai Kh——v; that Tsezar Markovich was modeled on the film director Lev Grossman; and that both Alyoshka the Baptist and Senka Klevshin could be related to actual prisoners.[13]

This reliance on real-life prototypes is a feature inherited from the Russian nineteenth-century literary tradition. In contrast to the Western tendency to draw a sharp distinction between fiction and non-fiction, the great Russian prose writers of the last century took pride in the way that their works addressed and reflected the actual historical, social, or moral conditions of their homeland. Literary achievement was not seen in the ability of a powerful imagination to create a vivid fictional world ex nihilo, but rather in the writer's skill in selecting, shaping, and ordering the data of reality, in this sense re-creating it in aesthetically compelling ways.[14]

Solzhenitsyn has been very explicit about his adherence to this tradition. When an interviewer noted that some readers perceive *One Day* as an essentially autobiographical work, he responded as follows: "There is nothing I can do about it, for I can really see no task higher than serving reality, that is, re-creating a reality trampled, destroyed, and maligned in our country. I do not consider invention as such to be my task or goal, and I never seek to dazzle my readers with my fancies. For a writer, invention is simply a means of concentrating reality."[15]

The author's intention is here stated with absolute clarity: *One Day in the Life of Ivan Denisovich* is a work that aspires in equal measure to cognitive, ethical, and aesthetic goals, doing so in a manner entirely free of self-conscious worries about artistic purity. Indeed it is appropriate to recall here that Solzhenitsyn's subtitle for *The Gulag Archipelago*, his monumental study of the system of Soviet prisons and camps, is "An Experiment in Literary Investigation," with literary art boldly proclaimed as a method in the pursuit of a cognitive goal. And although *One Day* is obviously far more modest in scope, the basic approach is very similar, depending as it does on the evocative power of art to create an indelible image of a long-hidden reality.[16]

One Day is packed with information about the grim world of Soviet forced-labor camps, a realm so remote from the experience of most modern readers that some historical commentary is required.

The time frame is specified precisely. It is early 1951 (40; *31*);[17] Stalin, referred to as "Old Man Whiskers" (158; *105*) is in power; and the Korean War is raging (157; *104*). The setting is a so-called Special Camp situated somewhere in Central Asia. Although various types of concentration and forced-labor camps were a feature of the Soviet system from the beginning of its existence, Special Camps were established by Stalin in 1948 for the purpose of segregating political prisoners from the allegedly far less threatening common criminals.[18] The number patches so prominently mentioned in the text were specific to Special Camps, as were other rules, such as a harsh limitation on the number of letters that inmates were permitted to write (two per year [40; *31*]), and the denial of even the token remuneration for work performed that was paid to inmates in most "ordinary" camps (156; *103*).

But confinement in a Special Camp had one paradoxical compensation. Because all the prisoners held there were automatically categorized as class enemies – in contrast to common criminals, who were viewed by the regime as "socially friendly"[19] – the camp administration seems to have made less of an effort to curtail the kind of "anti-Soviet" talk that would have swiftly led to dire consequences in other types of camps (158–59; *105*). While the security officer still depended on spies among the inmates – a man named Panteleyev is identified as a "squealer" in Shukhov's work gang (29; *23–24*) – we learn that a number of suspected collaborators have been murdered in the camp, with the result that the prisoners have become more outspoken (72, 105; *50, 71*). Thus we see Tyurin openly recounting the horrendous story of the injustices the regime had visited upon him and his family (88–93; *61–64*), while other zeks speak disrespectfully of Stalin (158; *105*) or argue loudly about the Korean War (157; *104*).[20]

The charges that led to the imprisonment of many of the inmates are identified; in most other cases one can easily guess. Shukhov had briefly fallen into German hands during the war and was immediately accused of being a German spy (70; *49*); the same kind of paranoid logic explains the ten-year sentence meted out to the former prisoner of war Yermolaev (150; *99*). Senka Klevshin and Captain Buynovsky were convicted of espionage for mere contact with foreigners: Senka had been liberated from a German concentration camp by the U.S. Army and had spent two days with the Americans, while the Captain had served briefly as a Soviet liaison officer on a British Navy vessel. This was deemed reason enough for both men to be charged with treason and slapped with twenty-five-year sentences (126; *84–85*). In fact, the camp held so many alleged spies that the only authentic one was regarded as a curiosity (120; *81*).

By 1951 Tyurin had served nineteen years in the camps for nothing more than having been a member of a family classified as *kulaks*, that is, peasants who had opposed – or were merely suspected of opposing – the policy of forced collectivization of agriculture launched in 1929 and implemented with unimaginable brutality in the early 1930s. Alyoshka and the other Baptists had been sentenced to twenty-five years for their faith alone (45; *33*).

Some differences do exist, however. Thus Pavlo, the deputy foreman of Gang 104, had been a member of the radical Ukrainian nationalist organization associated with the name of Stepan Bendera; the Benderites had carried out guerrilla-type attacks on Soviet installations in Ukraine for some years following the Second World War (95; *65*). In this respect Pavlo and several other Benderites referred to (15; *15*), together with the individual identified as a real spy, represent the tiny minority of prisoners in this camp whose sentences stemmed from genuinely hostile acts against the Soviet regime. No distinction between real and imaginary enemies existed in the mind of the regime, however, and the grotesquely disproportional nature of the system of punishment is further illustrated by the fact that the young teenager Gopchik received the same twenty-five-year sentence as the active Benderite partisans for the mere act of having taken milk to their forest hideout (63; *45*).

Significant characters whose charges are not specified but can be surmised from the context include the Estonians and the Latvians, tens of thousands of whom had been arrested in the crackdown on "bourgeois nationalism" aimed at individuals with ties to the pre-Soviet Baltic regimes and anyone else suspected of harboring hopes of national independence.[21] The filmmaker Tsezar Markovich was, in all likelihood, a victim of the purge of "rootless cosmopolites" (the codeword for Russian Jewish intellectuals) that took place in the Soviet Union in the late 1940s and early 1950s. We are also given a brief but memorable depiction of prisoner Yu-81, a man of unbowed spirit who is reputed to have been confined to prisons and camps for "as long as the Soviet state had existed" (154; *102*), perhaps for refusing to mask his contempt for the regime and the system it had instituted.

By peopling his text with a diverse gallery of prisoner types, the overwhelming majority of them sentenced to harsh terms for nonexistent crimes, and by taking care to endow these characters with life histories modeled on authentic biographies, Solzhenitsyn succeeded in evoking a picture that was at once shocking in its portrayal of massive injustice and true to the actual, but heretofore unacknowledged, experience of vast numbers of Soviet readers. For in 1962 the USSR was a country where tens of millions of citizens had either tasted of the camps themselves or had a relative or friend who did (who may never have returned), but where the very existence of these institutions could be mentioned in a work meant for publication or performance only in the most oblique or mendacious fashion. By addressing this taboo-ridden theme head-on, doing so, moreover, in a rich and sometimes earthy language that stood in dazzling contrast to the bland linguistic norms of the day, *One Day* could not fail to trigger powerful reactions among its readers. One might say that in the Soviet context, *One Day* performed a kind of "social therapy" (the phrase is Donald Fanger's[22]) by its irrefutable affirmation of reality, in this sense liberating readers from the stifling restrictions and evasions that had characterized officially sanctioned Soviet literature for decades. Indeed, as numerous commentators who witnessed the 1962 appearance of *One Day* in Moscow have attested, the depth of the public response was simply unprecedented, and unmatched by the reaction to any other literary event before or since.[23] It is a testament to the emotion of the moment, as well as to the writer's skill, that the sophisticated literary structure of this work appeared invisible to many readers, with the text perceived as a sort of eyewitness report. A vivid example of this misreading is cited by the Russian politician Grigori Yavlinsky, who recalls, as one of the memorable events of his life, his father's unhesitating assessment of *One Day*: "It is not literature at all," he declared to the young Grigori, who had been perplexed by this work. "It is simply the truth."[24]

Though clearly intended as a positive evaluation of Solzhenitsyn's text, the elder Yavlinsky's words would have been utterly unacceptable to the author. Within the Russian tradition to which Solzhenitsyn belongs, there is no sympathy for the view of literature as a self-indulgent or merely decorative activity unrelated to truthtelling. It is assumed that the writer's God-given talent must not be wasted on idle fancies at a time when he is a witness to the pains and sorrows of his society. Yet at the same time the writer is called on to adhere to the principles of literary art, thereby avoiding any nakedly utilitarian or propagandistic agenda. The ideal is a fusion of a subject matter of high seriousness with an aesthetic structure appropriate to it.

Solzhenitsyn's *One Day in the Life of Ivan Denisovich* is proof that such a goal is attainable. As the writer indicates in the statements cited earlier, his intention of describing the world of the labor camps was, from the beginning, cast in terms of a search for a suitable narrative form. He would, he had decided, base it on a detailed account of the events of a single day. More important, he had chosen to present the camp experience largely, though not entirely, through the consciousness, and in the language, of an uneducated peasant prisoner, all the while retaining the third-person mode. This kind of narrative is technically known as *erlebte Rede*, and Dorrit Cohn, who has proposed "narrated monologue" as an English equivalent of the German phrase, offers the following succinct definition of the technique: "rendering a character's thought in his own idiom while maintaining the third-person reference and the basic tense of narration."[25] This technique shares with first-person narrative the ability to present a markedly subjective view of the world in unmediated fashion, with the self-characterization that this automatically entails, but takes the crucial further step of rendering the subjective point of view in a grammatical form ordinarily associated with objective narration. In theory, this permits the writer to shuttle easily between the individual perspective of a particular character and the more impartial language of a general narrator, each time without any explicit signals of the shift. In the case of *One Day*, however, positing any general narrator separate from Ivan Shukhov is problematic because the subjective statements that can be unambiguously linked to Shukhov are expressed in the same substandard lexical medium as the more neutral descriptive passages. Illustrations can be drawn from virtually any page of the text, although this feature can often be partially obscured in the English version owing to the difficulty of reproducing the nuances of nonliterary Russian in a credible English form. The following example is representative of each of these points:

> [Shukhov] took a hatchet and a brush for the ice [*dlia lëdu*], his gavel [*molotochek kamenotësnyi*], his pole, his cord, and a plumb line.
>
> Red-faced Kildigs gave Shukhov a sour look – why jump up before the foreman? It was all right for Kildigs – he didn't have to worry where the gang's next meal was coming from [because he received food parcels – A. K.]: two hundred grams of bread more or less didn't matter to the bald-headed so-and-so. (94; *64*)

While the first sentence in this passage is essentially descriptive and lacks the judgmental tone of the phrases immediately following, it contains a conspicuous instance of ungrammatical usage (*dlia lëdu* instead of *dlia l'da*), as well as a lexical inversion (*molotochek kamenotësnyi*) that suggests popular style. Although one could argue on the basis of such passages that Shukhov's explicitly subjective narration (as in "the bald-headed so-and-so") is interspersed with the voice of a different and more neutral narrator, one who happens to share Shukhov's linguistic traits, it would seem that drawing these distinctions contributes nothing to an understanding of the text as a whole.[26] The crucial point, rather, is that *One Day* provides virtually uninterrupted commentary on the camp experience from what might be called a generically peasant perspective. In this sense, Shukhov's individual voice is simply a particularly expressive form of a modality that dominates the text.

Before addressing the significance of this viewpoint it is important to note that Solzhenitsyn has provided three-dot ellipses to mark the beginning and end of three descriptive passages that depart from anything Shukhov – or the generalized peasant narrator – could have seen or heard. Appropriately, each of these three texts is presented in the standard "educated" literary style, a format that diverges sharply from the idiom used in the rest of *One Day*. The first of these passages explains the activities of a medical orderly whose interest in writing poetry is "nothing that Shukhov would have comprehended"(23; *19*), the second gives us a brief insight into Tsezar's mind as he smokes "to set his mind racing in pursuit of some idea" (31; *25*), and the third allows us to glimpse Buynovsky's psychological state as he begins to evolve from "a loud and domineering naval officer into a slow-moving and circumspect zek" (82; *57*).[27]

Apart from these three instances, the text of *One Day* does not provide any explicit signals for distinguishing narrative voices, and Shukhov's mental verbalizations are seamlessly followed by utterances of others spoken in his presence, even when the subject is something he obviously cannot understand, as when he is a silent presence during Tsezar's "educated conversation" about Eisenstein (85; *59*). The typographical markers, then, serve to separate out only those passages where Shukhov (and the generalized peasant consciousness for which he stands) could not be considered either a witness or a commentator.[28]

The significance of the peasant viewpoint for a reading of *One Day* has received considerable attention in the critical literature. Some commentators have argued that by relying so heavily on this perspective, Solzhenitsyn has imposed undesirable restraints on his text, since Shukhov's intellectual limitations render him incapable of grasping, let alone articulating, the full implications of what he sees.[29] One response to this criticism has been to contend that the writer's decision to show us a Stalinist labor camp through the deliberately narrowed focus of Shukhov's consciousness forces us to confront this material directly, without the opportunity of escaping into intellectual rationalizations.[30] In particular, I would add, it makes it virtually impossible to read *One Day* as an illustration of the meaninglessness of life – that ultimately facile modern response to the special horrors of the twentieth century. This is so because a central feature of Shukhov's peasant nature is an indestructibly firm grip on reality, manifested throughout the text by his clear-eyed observations and sensible commentaries. Thus Shukhov acknowledges the *ability* of the powers that be to crush all open resistance (e.g., 52; *38*), and because he prizes survival above proud resistance (70; *49*), he submits to the external rules imposed on him. Yet he concedes nothing more to a system whose brutality and flagrant lies remain perfectly obvious to him. The camp we see through Shukhov's eyes is a place of organized malevolence and willfully enforced perversity, not an incomprehensible product of undirected chaos.[31]

Shukhov demonstrates his sturdy sense of moral orientation in a number of other ways as well. Though he is obviously focused on day-to-day survival, we learn, for example, that he has nevertheless asked his wife not to send him food parcels because he understands how much his family would have to sacrifice for his sake (139; *93*). He is unfailingly honest in his dealings with fellow prisoners, conscientious to a fault in his attitude toward work, and has managed to maintain his human dignity in the degrading circumstances of the camp.

In contrast, the two intellectually developed characters in Shukhov's work gang, Captain Buynovsky and Tsezar Markovich, both exhibit behavior that demonstrates a degree of blindness to the reality of the camp world. Thus the overbearing Buynovsky, who believes himself to be vastly superior to Shukhov in terms of general understanding (e.g., 116; *78*), has not absorbed the evidence of injustice and corruption that surrounds him on all sides, and in his protest during the morning search seems genuinely convinced that "real Soviet people" must, by definition, be fair, and that, furthermore, the camp authorities do not know the Criminal Code (35; *27*). Shukhov demurs silently ("It's you, brother, who don't know anything yet!"). Later in the day Buynovsky appears to be equally sincere in professing his faith in Soviet laws (126; *85*), a statement that causes Shukhov to mutter a vigorously skeptical comment to himself.

In the case of Tsezar Markovich, Shukhov's criticism is expressed less directly. Tsezar, who has been able to avoid the physical labor of the other members of his work gang thanks to his food parcels (which he uses to bribe the administrators), seems naively unaware of the moral insensitivity he displays in his preoccupation with aesthetic categories. It is particularly troubling to hear a prisoner of Stalin's police state, set as he is among other innocent victims of indiscriminate repression, extolling a cinematic sequence in which Eisenstein has aestheticized the *oprichniki*, Ivan the Terrible's murderous private army (85; 59).[32] And although Shukhov is a silent and presumably uncomprehending witness of this tribute to Eisenstein, the scene is structured to emphasize Tsezar's self-absorption: Tsezar reaches out for the bowl of gruel that Shukhov has saved for him with some effort without even acknowledging Shukhov's presence. For all he knows, "the gruel might have traveled through the air unaided" (86; 59).[33]

Apart from Buynovsky and Tsezar, the only other intellectual figure with whom Shukhov has dealings during his day is the medical orderly Vdovushkin. A mild-mannered former literature student who in his present capacity has only minimal authority to grant ailing prisoners dispensation from the regular workday, Vdovushkin is shown as so engrossed in his poetry writing that his advice to Shukhov to report for work as usual, though entirely reasonable under the circumstances, nevertheless contains an unmistakable note of indifference. Indeed it is this nuance that causes Shukhov to get to his feet abruptly and stalk out the door without so much as a nod to Vdovushkin (24; 20). The moral overtones of this episode are thereupon made explicit in a rhetorical question that immediately follows Shukhov's departure: "Can a man who's warm understand one who's freezing?" (Tëplyi ziablogo razve kogda poimët?) (ibid.). The laconic and distinctly nonliterary style of the Russian phrase adds aphoristic punch and serves as a particularly clear example of the unfailing sense of reality typical of Shukhov and the peasant mentality that he represents. It is also a good illustration of a point articulated by Tvardovsky, the editor of *Novy Mir*, at the time of his first meeting with Solzhenitsyn. *One Day*, he proclaimed, is a new departure in Russian literature in the sense that intellectuals are viewed through the eyes of the common people, and not vice versa as had been the custom.[34]

Solzhenitsyn has maintained that this aspect of his text was a decisive, albeit unanticipated, factor in its publication history. Indeed we know that the manuscript copy of *One Day* was able to attract Tvardovsky's attention by virtue of a comment strategically dropped in his presence to the effect that the work was about "a prison camp as seen through the eyes of a peasant."[35] The point here is that Tvardovsky was of peasant origin, as was the mercurial Nikita Khrushchev, and Solzhenitsyn believes that Khrushchev's decision to allow *One Day* to be published in the Soviet Union's leading literary magazine, as Tvardovsky had so assiduously urged him to do, was directly influenced by the instinctively positive reaction of both men to the peasant outlook expressed by Shukhov. As Solzhenitsyn puts it, "I cannot say that I had precisely planned it, but I did accurately foresee that the muzhik [i.e., peasant – A. K.] Ivan Denisovich was bound to arouse sympathy in the superior muzhik Tvardovsky and the supreme muzhik Nikita Khrushchev."[36]

Solzhenitsyn has gone on to suggest that this same quality may account for the fact that *One Day* did not surface in the West during the several months in 1962 when it circulated in typewritten copies while awaiting publication in *Novy Mir*: "The work was too peasant-oriented, too Russian, and hence as it were encoded. If Western correspondents did read the samizdat version at the time, they probably judged it to have limited appeal to Western tastes."[37]

One need not share the writer's belief that a special effort is needed to understand Shukhov's perspective to appreciate that Solzhenitsyn is referring to the Russian nineteenth-century tradition of invoking the "common people" as the bearers of moral virtue.[38]

Solzhenitsyn's own attitude to this tradition is ambivalent. In his novel *The First Circle*, a chapter is dedicated to tracing the evolving views on this subject held by Gleb Nerzhin, the novel's main protagonist.[39] In his struggle to understand what in the nineteenth century had become an almost obsessive Russian question, Nerzhin befriends the peasant janitor Spiridon and attempts to grasp what motivates his behavior. Predictably enough he concludes that Spiridon is no font of wisdom who could provide guidance in the complex world of the present, but he nevertheless finds much to admire in the janitor's unwavering attachment to his family and in his home-spun moral criteria.

A much more significant variation on this theme is provided by "Matryona's Home," a short story Solzhenitsyn began writing during a pause in his work on *One Day*. The heroine of the story's title is an aging peasant woman whose virtues are so obscured by the squalor of her surroundings that they become apparent only after her death. It is a symptom of the prevailing moral climate that she is an anomaly in her village, derided by fellow peasants for her impractical selflessness and beset by shamelessly greedy relatives. Though constantly humiliated and unrecognized during her life, Matryona emerges, in the words of a Russian proverb (which served as the original title of the story), as that "righteous one without whom no village can stand." Solzhenitsyn clearly views her as an embodiment of the moral ideal championed by the earlier tradition, so that the very fact of her existence constitutes proof of the survival of these values among the degradations of Soviet life.

Situated chronologically between the writing of *The First Circle* and "Matryona's Home," *One Day* naturally enough reflects some of the thematic concerns addressed in both. To begin with, there is a partial but unmistakable parallel between Spiridon and Shukhov. Although the protagonist of *One Day* is incomparably more conscious of the world than the blind janitor depicted in *The First Circle*, he shares with Spiridon such crucial traits as an unwavering adherence to a firm but somewhat idiosyncratic code of behavior and a seemingly complete immunity to ideological thinking. But as a minor character in *The First Circle*, Spiridon receives only limited attention in the novel, and the analogy noted here is schematic rather than substantial.

The continuity between *One Day* and "Matryona's Home" is of far greater import. This is so despite the obvious fact that the value Shukhov consciously assigns to survival is at odds with Matryona's instinctive selflessness, and that, furthermore, the external portrayal of Matryona stands in contrast to the direct transcript of Shukhov's thoughts in *One Day*. The similarity lies in the sustained focus of both texts on protagonists whose actions and attitudes are taken to express certain moral qualities residual in the Russian peasant mentality. It is at this point that the central premise of the Russian nineteenth-century tradition comes into play: it is assumed that what is being depicted can, in some essential way, be viewed as representative of genuine social or historical reality, rather than expressing a creative vision that lacks any obvious relation to the world of ordinary experience. In these terms, all of Solzhenitsyn's works are firmly within the realistic tradition: the writer has taken pains to suggest the typicality of a figure such as Shukhov in the labor camps of the postwar Soviet Union, and in the case of "Matryona's Home" he informs us, in the annotation to the story, that the life and death of his heroine are described "exactly as they happened."[40]

The plight of the peasantry as a social class is also thematically present in both texts, albeit only obliquely so in "Matryona's Home." This theme becomes very explicit in *One Day*, where apart from Tyurin's harrowing tale of the terroristic methods by which collectivization was implemented (esp. 93; *64*), we are given Shukhov's melancholy thoughts on the catastrophic state of the kolkhoz in his village (42; *31*) as well as his recollection of agricultural abundance in pre-collectivization times (50; *36*).

What Solzhenitsyn is suggesting, ultimately, is that individuals such as Shukhov, Tyurin, and Matryona represent real personality types that have not been extirpated from the national psyche in spite of the devastations of Soviet history. No matter how precarious the survival of these characters is shown to be, the very fact that Solzhenitsyn finds such qualities as honesty, clearheadedness, tough resilience, and even Christian meekness operative in the conditions he describes is tantamount to an assertion of faith in the enduring spirit of the Russian peasant. It is a sentiment that Shukhov is allowed to articulate toward the end of his long day as he manages to draw some pleasure from a bowl of the miserable mush that serves as his supper: "We shall survive. We shall survive it all. God willing, we'll see the end of it!" (153; *101*). It seems appropriate to conclude that here Shukhov is giving voice to a hope shared by an author who, in another context, has stated that he considers himself to be "a peasant at heart."[41]

Another aspect of *One Day* that has been the subject of considerable discussion is Shukhov's attitude toward work. Shukhov is a former carpenter who clearly enjoys working with his hands and is so adept at various practical tasks that he is considered one of the two most skilled workmen in Gang 104 (55; *40*). At the same time, his instinctively positive view of work is sharply delimited by the abnormal circumstances of the camp world: he is disgusted to hear that the new camp doctor has been burdening his patients with physical tasks in the cynical belief that this is the best kind of therapy (23; *19*), and he is convinced that when one works directly for the bosses (as when he is made to clean the floor in the guard room), one is fully justified in doing a sloppy job (14; *14*).

Not surprisingly, however, the most significant aspects of Shukhov's attitude emerge from his actions and feelings rather than from any explicit generalizations on his part. We note, first, that deep involvement in practical tasks serves Shukhov as a way of temporarily escaping the consciousness of his environment. When he undertakes to attach a piece of chimney pipe to the stove in the building site, for example, "every other thought went clean out of his head. He had no memory, no concern for anything except how he was going to join the lengths of pipe and fix them so that the stove would not smoke" (61; *44*).

For Shukhov work is what makes time fly by (67; *47*) (although, as he adds bitterly, one's sentence does not seem to get shorter for it). It is also what helps him forget the aches and pains that troubled him in the morning (128; *86*).

But the central episode involving the philosophy of work is of course the lengthy description of Shukhov and his fellow prisoners engaged in building a wall (94–113; *64–77*). This scene was singled out for praise by Nikita Khrushchev and dismissed by several early readers as typical socialist realism.[42] In each case the judgment is based on the belief that Shukhov's obvious dedication to doing a good job and the satisfaction he experiences can be equated with the so-called labor enthusiasm that had become a stock component in an endless series of Soviet novels lauding "socialist construction."

One example drawn from an influential early novel will suffice to characterize this particular genre. Gleb Chumalov, the hero of *Cement* (1925), is shown with a multitude of other workers during their common effort to restore a ruined factory: "It was not the support of individuals that Gleb felt, but rather the combined power of the masses around him. Bathed in perspiration he worked like a bull . . . This brute strength . . . flowed upon him in great waves through the thunder of the earth, across the stones and rails, from the enormous ant-like crowd."[43] The emphasis here, as elsewhere in *Cement*, is on Gleb Chumalov's ecstatic loss of individuality as he merges with a proletarian mass inspired by the communist vision. In the quasi-religious world of this archetypal Soviet production novel, Gleb must jettison his personal sentiments and ambitions in the process of acquiring the higher awareness mystically embodied in the Party.

Nothing remotely similar occurs in *One Day*. To begin with, it hardly needs to be stated that neither Shukhov not any members of his work gang are toiling for the greater glory of communism. They are forced laborers whose food rations *as a group* are directly linked to whatever production norms have been set for them (61–63; *43–45*); the rampant use of bribes to modify the effects of this rule clearly has its limits. Yet it is obvious that in the process of building the wall, several members of Gang 104 become caught up in the activity in a way that cannot be ascribed to the need to fulfill some externally imposed quota. The motivation is profoundly internal in origin, entailing what is perhaps the most significant means of self-expression available to prisoners in the coercive environment of the camp. Good workmanship here becomes a source of professional pride and self-esteem, and Shukhov's thoughts as he inspects his handiwork before dashing off to catch up with his work gang offer a particularly clear example of this phenomenon. The context is all important. Shukhov is already risking punishment by staying a few minutes past quitting time in order to finish putting down a row of cinder blocks. But he is driven by an inner compulsion to take the following extra step: "If the guards had set their dogs on him, it wouldn't have stopped Shukhov. He moved quickly back from the wall to take a good look. All right. Then quickly up to the wall to look over the top from left to right. Outside straight as could be. Hands weren't past it yet. Eye as good as any spirit level" (113; 77). It would be difficult to imagine a more explicit statement of the significance this job has acquired for Shukhov: it serves to reinforce his faith in himself as a competent human being.

In *The Gulag Archipelago* Solzhenitsyn acknowledges the paradoxical moral situation by virtue of which good work performed in the context of a closed and coercive system inevitably contributes to the system's strength, despite the psychological benefit it may bring the worker in the short run. But he vigorously rejects the arguments of those who would accuse him of glorifying slave labor in the wall-building episode. In his opinion, the issue ultimately comes down to survival: "How could Ivan Denisovich get through ten years if all he could do was curse his work day and night? . . . in that case he would have had to hang himself on the first handy hook!"[44]

The author then proceeds to tell us that he himself experienced the exhilaration of a job well done during his term in prison camp:

Such is man's nature that even bitter, detested work is sometimes performed with an incomprehensible wild excitement. Having worked for two years with my hands, I encountered this strange phenomenon myself: suddenly you become absorbed in the work itself, irrespective of whether it is slave labor and offers you nothing. I experienced those strange moments at bricklaying (otherwise I wouldn't have written about it), at foundry work, even in the fervor of breaking up old pig iron with a sledge. And so surely we can allow Ivan Denisovich not to feel his inescapable labor as a terrible burden forever, not to hate it perpetually?[45]

The tone of sobriety and common sense to which Solzhenitsyn gives voice here is further proof of the way in which the writer's own view of the world merges with that of his peasant protagonist.

Some comments are needed, finally, on the textual history of *One Day*, both in Russian and in English translation.

The typescript that was submitted to *Novy Mir* in late 1961 under the title of *Shch-854 (Odin den' odnogo zeka)* was a politically toned-down version of a text Solzhenitsyn had composed in 1959.[46] At a meeting with the magazine's editorial board in mid-December of that year, the author was asked to make a few relatively insignificant changes to which he agreed after some consideration; he also accepted Tvardovsky's proposal of a different title (*Odin den' Ivana Denisovicha*) as well as the suggestion that the work be labeled a "tale" (*povest'*) rather than a "short story" (*rasskaz*).[47] Some further changes were made in mid-1962 at the request of Khrushchev's adviser, Vladimir Lebedev,[48] before the text appeared in the November issue of *Novy Mir*.[49] *One Day* was published twice more in early 1963, first in a journal that specialized in reproducing recent fiction in mass editions printed on newspaper-quality paper,[50] and shortly thereafter in a hard-cover book edition produced by the Sovetskii pisatel' publishing house in Moscow.[51] Both these later editions diverge in some textual details from the *Novy Mir* version, but the differences are slight.[52]

The Russian text was never again published in the Soviet Union, and the next significant Russian-language edition of *One Day* appeared ten years later in Paris under the imprint of YMCA Press.[53] In a prefatory note to this edition, Solzhenitsyn declares the Paris publication to contain the definitive and final version of *One Day*, and Gary Kern, who has compared all textual variations among the four above-mentioned editions, concludes that the 1973 YMCA Press version restores many, but not necessarily all, of the passages deleted from the original manuscript entitled *Shch-854*. The Paris edition also retains some of the changes incorporated in the *Novy Mir* text.[54]

Five years later, when Solzhenitsyn launched his Russian-language *Collected Works*,[55] *One Day* appeared with a small number of further emendations, including the removal of the genre indicator *povest'* that had been featured in all four previous editions. It follows that only the text as published in the third volume of the *Collected Works* can be regarded as canonical.

The English-language versions of *One Day* must be grouped in accordance with this textual history. Of the six extant translations, five were based on the *Novy Mir* text. They are, in order of their appearance:

1. *One Day in the Life of Ivan Denisovich*, trans. Ralph Parker (New York: Dutton, 1963).[56]

2. ———, trans. Max Hayward and Ronald Hingley (New York: Praeger, 1963).

3. ———, trans. Bela Von Block (New York: Lancer, 1963).

4. ———, trans. Thomas P. Whitney (New York: Crest, 1963).

5. ———, trans. Gillon Aitken, rev. ed. (New York: Farrar Straus Giroux, 1971).

As I have argued elsewhere, the Hayward and Hingley translation, despite numerous faults, seems to be the most successful of these five versions in conveying the force of the original, and the Bela Von Block rendition must be ranked last in terms of reliability.[57] However, the question of rankings within this group of translations is ultimately moot for the simple reason that each is based on an outdated original.

The only English version of *One Day* that relies on the canonical Russian text is the translation by H. T. Willetts (New York: Noonday/Farrar Straus Giroux, 1991). Apart from being textually authoritative, the Willetts version is also superior to its predecessors in coping with the intricacies of the original Russian. A recent study on translation theory includes a comparative analysis of the way several translators, including Willetts, have rendered some passages from *One Day* into English. While the author of that study still finds plenty to criticize in the Willetts version, she judges it to represent a major improvement in rendering the subjective quality of the narrative voice that distinguishes the work.[58]

Earlier I mentioned the difficulty of finding credible English equivalents for the substandard grammatical forms and peasant intonations so prominent in *One Day*. It needs to be said that much of it is simply impossible to translate, even in theory. For, as Kornei Chukovsky has observed in a whimsical discussion on the translation of colloquial style, there really is no way of communicating in another language the tonalities of the southern Mississippi dialect spoken by the Negro Jim in Mark Twain's *Huckleberry Finn*.[59]

A similar problem is posed by Solzhenitsyn's liberal use of slightly veiled obscenities. All the early translators assumed that the euphemisms had been devised solely for the benefit of the prudish Soviet censors and that they could be safely ignored. But it turns out that Solzhenitsyn has left this feature virtually unchanged in the Russian-language editions of *One Day* published in the West. And in a footnote in the new edition of *The Oak and the Calf* he expresses his annoyance with those translators who rushed to use explicit four-letter words in place of what he calls his "hints at profanity" (namëki na bran').[60]

The problem seems unresolvable. English has only a few recognizable euphemisms of the "goldarn" type, but all are perceived as either so coy or so trite that their use would be unacceptably jarring in a text like *One Day*. Nor can a translator be reasonably expected to follow Solzhenitsyn in inventing new euphemisms for the English version of *One Day*: no copy editor would let that pass. The sad but inescapable truth is that the process of translation may involve losses that cannot be avoided. Minimizing these losses must be the eternal goal of every translator, but natural limits must be acknowledged.

NOTES

1. Aleksandr Solzhenitsyn, *Sobranie sochinenii*, 20 vols. (Vermont and Paris: YMCA Press, 1978–1991), 3:327. (The writer has demonstrated some uncertainty about the date. In a 1976 statement – "Interv'iu na literaturnye temy s N.A.Struve," *Sobranie sochinenii*, 10:518 – he speaks of this moment as having occurred in 1952, while in the BBC interview referred to in Note 2 he places it in 1950. One assumes that the date indicated in the annotation to the *Collected Works* is the most authoritative one.)

2. "Interv'iu dlia radio Bi-Bi-Si," *Vestnik Russkogo Khristianskogo Dvizheniia*, no. 138 (1983):155. For similar statements made on other occasions, see *Sobranie sochinenii*, 10: 518, and Solzhenitsyn's comments as quoted in Michael Scammell, *Solzhenitsyn: A Biography* (New York: Norton, 1984), p. 382.

3. Solzhenitsyn, *Sobranie sochinenii*, 7: 573.

4. The first of Solzhenitsyn's works to deal specifically with individuals arrested on political grounds is the play *Prisoners* (Plenniki, 1953). This was followed by *The Republic of Labor* (Respublika truda, 1954), a play set in a prison camp and available in English only in the abridged version entitled *The Love-Girl and the Innocent*. The next work in chronological terms was *The First Circle*, written in several versions starting in 1957; the setting is a prison research institute. A case could also be made for including the early play *Victory Celebrations* (Pir pobeditelei, 1951) in this series, since the plot revolves around the sinister presence of a SMERSH operative on the prowl for suspects. (The English translations of the plays *Victory Celebrations, Prisoners*, and *The Love-Girl and the Innocent* are available under one cover in a book published by Farrar Straus Giroux in 1986.)

5. Natalya A. Reshetovskaya, *Sanya: My Life with Aleksandr Solzhenitsyn*, trans. Elena Ivanoff (New York: Bobbs-Merrill, 1975), p. 211. Although the reminiscences of Solzhenitsyn's first wife must be used with caution, there seems no reason to question this particular piece of information.

6. "Interv'iu," *Vestnik R. Kh. D.*, no. 138, 155.

7. Solzhenitsyn, *Sobranie sochinenii*, 10:518.

8. "Interv'iu," *Vestnik R. Kh. D.*, no. 138, 155. Reshetovskaya writes that the starting and completion dates were May 18 and October 11, 1959, with the intervening summer months mostly taken up with other concerns (*Sanya*, p. 212).

9. Solzhenitsyn, *Sobranie sochinenii*, 3:327.

10. Solzhenitsyn, *Sobranie sochinenii*, 10:520.

11. Solzhenitsyn, *Sobranie sochinenii*, 10:520–21. For a different translation of this passage, see Aleksandr Solzhenitsyn, "An Interview with Nikita Struve," in John B. Dunlop, Richard S. Haugh, and Michael Nicholson, eds., *Solzhenitsyn in Exile: Critical Essays and Documentary Materials* (Stanford, Calif.: Hoover Institution Press, 1985), pp. 307–8.

12. Solzhenitsyn, *Sobranie sochinenii*, 3:327.

13. On Buynovsky, see *Current Digest of the Soviet Press* 16, no. 3 (Feb. 12, 1964): 12–13; and Solzhenitsyn, *The Gulag Archipelago*, 3 vols., trans. Thomas P. Whitney (vols. 1 and 2) and H. T. Willetts (vol. 3) (New York: Harper and Row, 1974–78), 3:54, 76. On Tyurin, see ibid., 3:365. Alyoshka's real-life equivalent is also mentioned in the *Current Digest* piece. The Tsezar Markovich–Lev Grossman connection is noted by Vladimir Lakshin in his *"Novyi mir" vo vremena Khrushcheva: Dnevnik i poputnoe (1953–1964)* (Moscow: Knizhnaia palata, 1991), p. 191. On Senka, see Dimitri Panin, *The Notebooks of Sologdin*, trans. John Moore (New York: Harcourt Brace Jovanovich, 1976), p. 310.

14. For a more detailed discussion, see Alexis Klimoff, "In Defense of the Word: Lydia Chukovskaya and the Russian Tradition," introduction to Lydia Chukovskaya, *The Deserted House*, trans. Aline Werth (Belmont, Mass.: Nordland, 1978), pp. i–xliv.

15. Solzhenitsyn, *Sobranie sochinenii*, 10: 519–520.

16. Nadezhda Mandelshtam has stated that no other work, not even any by Shalamov, was able to convey the tangible reality of the labor camps to the extent achieved by *One Day*. See her *Hope Abandoned*, trans. Max Hayward (New York: Atheneum, 1974), p. 612.

17. The parenthetical page references are, respectively, to the English translation of *One Day in the Life of Ivan Denisovich* by H. T. Willetts (New York: Noonday/ Farrar Straus Giroux, 1991), and to the canonical Russian text published in volume 3 (1978) of the twenty-volume *Sobranie sochinenii* (Vermont and Paris: YMCA Press, 1978–1991). The references to the Russian text are given in italics.

18. See Solzhenitsyn, *The Gulag Archipelago*, 3:34–35.

19. See, for example, Solzhenitsyn, *The Gulag Archipelago*, 2:425–46. The terminology is based on a class analysis performed in accordance with Marxist theory.

20. The references to the killing of informers were removed from the

manuscript Solzhenitsyn submitted to *Novy Mir*; they were reinserted into the restored versions published by the author in the West in 1973 and 1978.

21. One exception is Shukhov's Estonian campmate who had been arrested as a foreign spy when he naively returned to Estonia from Sweden (51; 37).

22. See Donald Fanger, "Solzhenitsyn: Art and Foreign Matter," in John B. Dunlop, Richard S. Haugh, and Alexis Klimoff, eds., *Aleksandr Solzhenitsyn: Critical Essays and Documentary Materials*, 2d ed. (New York and London: Collier Macmillan, 1975), p. 162.

23. See, for example, Raisa Orlova, *Vospominaniia o neproshedshem vremeni* (Moscow: Slovo, 1993), p. 221; and Mark Alt'shuller and Elena Dryzhakova, *Put' otrecheniia: Russkaia literatura 1953–1968* (Tenafly, N.J.: Ermitazh, 1985), p. 158. One detail will serve as an illustration of the prevailing atmosphere. The great poet Anna Akhmatova, who had read *One Day* in manuscript, delayed her departure to her home in Leningrad so that she could see the text in print. She would not leave Moscow, she said, "until I hold the November issue of *Novy Mir* in my hands" (see Lidiia Chukovskaia, *Zapiski ob Anne Akhmatovoi*, 2 vols. [Paris: YMCA Press, 1976–1980], 2:464).

24. Interview with Yavlinsky quoted in "Rossiia posle vyborov," *Russkaia mysl'* (Paris), August 1–7, 1996: ii (supplement).

25. Dorrit Cohn, *Transparent Minds: Narrative Modes for Presenting Consciousness in Fiction* (Princeton, N.J.: Princeton University Press, 1978), p. 100. Other critics have proposed different nomenclature, including "indirect interior monologue" and "represented discourse." The Russian equivalent of *erlebte Rede* is *nesobstvenno-priamaia rech'* or *kosvenno-priamaia rech'*.

26. Vladimir J. Rus admits that there is a "merging" of the two voices. See his "*One Day in the Life of Ivan Denisovich*: A Point of View Analysis," *Canadian Slavonic Papers* 13, nos. 2–3 (1971): 165–178.

27. The writer has also inserted an ellipsis at the beginning of Tyurin's account (88; 61), but this seems to be nothing more than an indication that Shukhov has not heard the beginning of the story.

28. *One Day* contains one other small paragraph of this general type relating to Buynovsky. (The text begins with "A guilty smile" [83; 57].) The paragraph was marked off with ellipses in the original *Novy Mir* version (*Novyi mir*, 1962, no. 11: 38) but no longer has this feature in the *Collected Works* edition, presumably because this text entails an external description that could be ascribed to Shukhov.

29. Victor Erlich seems to have been the first Western critic to formulate such a point of view. See his essay "Post-Stalin Trends in Russian Literature," *Slavic Review* 23, no. 3 (September 1964): 410. This argument has been echoed by numerous later critics in the West.

30. This position was articulated by Max Hayward in response to Victor Erlich's remarks, in "Solzhenitsyn's Place in Contemporary Soviet Literature," *Slavic Review* 23, no. 3 (September 1964): 435–36. Solzhenitsyn's own remarks on his rationale are quoted in Scammell's biography (see *Solzhenitsyn*, pp. 425–26).

31. This clearly also reflects the author's own sense of reality. See Joseph Frank's penetrating remarks in "From Gogol to the Gulag," in his *Through the Russian Prism: Essays on Literature and Culture* (Princeton, N.J.: Princeton University Press, 1990), p. 105.

32. This point is forcefully argued by L. Toker in "On Some Aspects of the Narrative Method in *One Day in the Life of Ivan Denisovich*," in W. Moskovich, ed., *Russian Philology & History: In Honor of Professor Victor Levin* (Jerusalem: Hebrew University, 1992), p. 277.

33. Readers of Tolstoy will recognize a striking analogy to the depiction of Napoleon at Tilsit in *War and Peace* (pt. 5, ch. 21 in the Garnett translation; Book 5, ch. 18, in the Maude translation).

34. Quoted in Scammell, *Solzhenitsyn*, p. 416.

35. Aleksandr Solzhenitsyn, *The Oak and the Calf: Sketches of Literary Life in the Soviet Union*, trans. H. T. Willetts (New York: Harper and Row, 1980), p. 20. This is confirmed by Viktor Nekrasov, who heard the story directly from Tvardovsky. See his "Isaichu . . . ," *Kontinent*, no. 18 (1978): 4 (special supplement).

36. Solzhenitsyn, *The Oak and the Calf*, p. 21. It goes without saying that Solzhenitsyn was also aware that Khrushchev intended to use *One Day* as a political weapon in his ongoing struggle for control of the Party. He addresses this point in the BBC interview, for example (see *Vestnik R. Kh. D.*, no. 138 [1983]: 158). But it is curious to note that in the memoirs Khrushchev dictated after his removal from power, the former First Secretary of the Party downplays this aspect and stresses his humanitarian intentions (see *Khrushchev Remembers: The Glasnost Tapes*, trans. and ed. Jerrold L. Schecter and Vyacheslav V. Luchkov [Boston: Little, Brown, 1990], pp. 196–99).

37. Aleksandr Solzhenitsyn, *Invisible Allies*, trans. Alexis Klimoff and Mi-

chael Nicholson (Washington, D.C.: Counterpoint, 1995), p. 127. On the extent of the manuscript's circulation, see Solzhenitsyn, *The Oak and the Calf*, p. 388.

38. In Russian literature, the most familiar examples are such depictions of peasants as Platon Karataev in Tolstoy's *War and Peace* or the servant Gerasim in the same author's "The Death of Ivan Ilyich." For an excellent survey of this tradition, see Cathy A. Frierson, *Peasant Icons: Representations of Rural People in Late Nineteenth-Century Russia* (New York: Oxford University Press, 1993). The alleged similarity between Shukhov and Karataev was a staple of negative Soviet criticism of *One Day*. Such an analogy is disputed by Christopher Moody, *Solzhenitsyn* (New York: Barnes and Noble, 1973), p. 40; and Mariia Shneerson, *Aleksandr Solzhenitsyn: Ocherki tvorchestva* (Frankfurt a/M: Posev, 1984), pp. 113–17.

39. The chapter is entitled "Going to the People," which in this case is an ironic usage of the nineteenth-century slogan made famous by the Russian populists (*narodniki*).

40. Solzhenitsyn, *Sobranie sochinenii*, 3: 327. Solzhenitsyn has published a photograph of Matryona standing in front of her house, in this sense indicating just how literally he means this statement. See Aleksandr Solzhenitsyn, *Bodalsia telenok s dubom*, 2d ed. (Moscow: Soglasie, 1996), fifth unnumbered page of photographs following p. 162.

41. Solzhenitsyn, *The Gulag Archipelago*, 2:281. In an interesting essay, Mariia Shneerson has argued that Solzhenitsyn intermittently adopts a tone of voice remarkably similar to Shukhov's in a number of his later works, including *The Gulag Archipelago* and *The Oak and the Calf* (see her "Golos Shukhova v proizvedeniiakh Solzhenitsyna," *Grani*, no. 146 [1987]: 106–33).

42. Khrushchev was particularly pleased with the way Shukhov had taken care to use up all the mortar that had been prepared for him (see Solzhenitsyn, *Bodalsia telenok s dubom*, 2d ed., p. 66). Among early readers the analogy to socialist realism was suggested by Lev Kopelev and Ilya Ehrenburg (see Lakshin, *"Novy mir" vo vremena Khrushcheva*, pp. 56, 88). Victor Erlich has echoed this sentiment by suggesting an analogy with the Soviet production novel (see his reply to Max Hayward in *Slavic Review* 23, no. 3 [September 1964]: 440).

43. F. V. Gladkov, *Cement*, trans. A. S. Arthur and S. Ashleigh (New York: Frederick Ungar, 1971), p. 135.

44. Solzhenitsyn, *The Gulag Archipelago*, 2: 258.

45. Ibid., p. 259. Solzhenitsyn spoke in a similar vein in a 1976 interview on French television (see *Sobranie sochinenii*, 10:300). At the same time it is important to note the bitterness that informs Solzhenitsyn's poem "The Mason" where he reflects on the perversity of his role in the construction of a camp jail (see *The Gulag Archipelago*, 3:74). For additional discussion of this theme, including a helpful reference to "The Bridge on the River Kwai," see Gary Kern, "Ivan the Worker," *Modern Fiction Studies* 23, no. 1 (Spring 1977): 27–30. Note further that even Varlam Shalamov, an adamant opponent of justifying work in the context of forced labor, admits that "it is possible that some people were saved by being carried away by their work" (see his 1962 letter to Solzhenitsyn in *Shalamovskii sbornik*, vyp. 1 [Vologda: Institut povysheniia kvalifikatsii, 1994], p. 68).

46. Solzhenitsyn, *Sobranie sochinenii*, 3:327; and his *The Oak and the Calf*, pp. 13, 24.

47. Solzhenitsyn, *The Oak and the Calf*, pp. 24–25. The title change was permanent, but Solzhenitsyn considered the change in genre designation a mistake (as he spells out in a footnote in *The Oak and the Calf*, p. 24), and in the Russian-language *Collected Works* he has included *One Day* in a volume subtitled "*Rasskazy*" (Stories). At the same time, Solzhenitsyn has occasionally used the designation *povest'* (tale) when speaking of *One Day* as originally published, for example in *Bodalsia telenok s dubom*, 2d ed., p. 477.

48. Solzhenitsyn, *The Oak and the Calf*, pp. 39–40.

49. *Novyi mir* 1962, no. 11: 8–74.

50. *Roman-gazeta* 1963, no. 1: 1–47.

51. A. Solzhenitsyn, *Odin den' Ivana Denisovicha. Povest'* (Moscow: Sovetskii pisatel', 1963), 144 pp. A tiny run of a Russian edition in Braille is also reported to have been published that year in Moscow; see Michael Nicholson, "Solzhenitsyn in 1981: A Bibliographical Reorientation," in Dunlop, Haugh, and Nicholson, eds., *Solzhenitsyn in Exile: Critical Essays and Documentary Materials*, p. 358.

52. See Gary Kern, "Solzhenitsyn's Self-Censorship: The Canonical Text of *Odin den' Ivana Denisovicha*," *Slavic and East European Journal* 20, no. 4 (1976): 421–36.

53. A. Solzhenitsyn, *Odin den' Ivana Denisovicha. Matrenin dvor* (Paris: YMCA Press, 1973).

54. Kern, "Solzhenitsyn's Self-Censorship," p. 430.

55. Solzhenitsyn, *Sobranie sochinenii. One Day* appears in volume 3 (1978).

56. Because the Soviet Union at the time was not yet a signatory of the International Copyright Convention, translations of interesting works published in the USSR were rushed into print in the West with the goal of "cornering the market" before any possible competition. The translation of *One Day* by Hayward and Hingley eventually came out on the very same day as Parker's version, and the unseemly race between the two editions was noted by many commentators (see, for example, the review by Harrison Salisbury in *The New York Times*, January 22, 1963, p. 7).

57. Alexis Klimoff, "Solzhenitsyn in English: An Evaluation," in Dunlop, Haugh, and Klimoff, eds., *Aleksandr Solzhenitsyn: Critical Essays and Documentary Materials*, 2d ed., pp. 614–20.

58. Rachel May, *The Translator in the Text: On Reading Russian Literature in English* (Evanston, Ill.: Northwestern University Press, 1994), pp. 47–48; see also pp. 80, 83, 92–93, 123–27, and 133.

59. Lauren G. Leighton, ed. and trans., *The Art of Translation: Kornei Chukovsky's "A High Art"* (Knoxville: University of Tennessee Press, 1984), p. 126.

60. Solzhenitsyn, *Bodalsia telnok s dubom*, 2d ed., p. 54. Solzhenitsyn also reports here that English translations of *One Day* were withdrawn from some school districts in Vermont and Massachusetts because of the raw language.

Aleksandr Solzhenitsyn: A Chronology of Important Dates

1918   December 11: Aleksandr Solzhenitsyn is born in Kislovodsk,
        a small town north of the Caucasus Mountains. His father, a
        demobilized artillery officer who had been a student at
        Moscow University before dropping out to enlist during
        World War I, was killed in a hunting accident six months
        before Aleksandr's birth. His mother, née Taissia Shcherbak,
        is the daughter of a wealthy Ukrainian farmer whose land
        and property would shortly be expropriated by the
        Bolsheviks.

1924   Taissia Solzhenitsyn moves to Rostov-on-Don with her son,
        where she experiences great economic privation owing to a
        policy of discrimination against relatives of former officers
        and landowners.

1936   The future writer graduates from secondary school and
        enrolls in Rostov University, where he specializes in physics
        and mathematics. His excellent academic record is now
        united with an ardent belief in Marxist-Leninist doctrine.

1939   While continuing his studies in physics and mathematics,
        Solzhenitsyn enrolls in a correspondence course in literature
        at the Moscow Institute of Philosophy, Literature, and
        History (MIFLI).

1940   He marries fellow student Natalia Reshetovskaya.

1941   Solzhenitsyn graduates from Rostov University and completes
        MIFLI course. Further study of literature in Moscow is
        planned but made impossible by the outbreak of war with
        Germany in June. His attempt to enlist fails when he is
        rejected on medical grounds. In October, however, he is
        nevertheless called up for army service in the rear.

1942   He completes an accelerated course for artillery officers, is commissioned, and is placed in command of an observation battery, a unit engaged in determining the location of enemy artillery by means of sound ranging.

1943–45   He sees major action on the front lines, is twice decorated for personal bravery and promoted to captain.

1945   February 9: Solzhenitsyn is arrested at the front for critical comments about Stalin in correspondence with a friend. He is brought to Moscow under guard and summarily sentenced to eight years hard labor with subsequent "perpetual exile."

1945–46   He is confined in a labor camp of the "ordinary" kind, where political prisoners are mixed with common criminals. His Marxist faith is badly shaken.

1946–50   Thanks to his scientific training, Solzhenitsyn is transferred to a prison research institute of the type described in *The First Circle*. His ideological evolution continues.

1950–53   He is confined in a Special Camp (for political prisoners only) in Kazakhstan. The living and working conditions in this labor camp are reflected in *One Day in the Life of Ivan Denisovich*. Solzhenitsyn secretly composes and memorizes thousands of lines of verse. The Christian faith he imbibed in childhood is rekindled.

1953–56   Release from prison camp on the day of Stalin's death (March 5, 1953) is followed by compulsory exile to Kok Terek, a small Kazakh settlement. Solzhenitsyn teaches mathematics and physics in a local school but uses every scrap of free time for writing. Cancer is diagnosed in late 1953 and pronounced to be terminal, but the writer is successfully treated in a Tashkent clinic in 1954–55. (His illness and treatment are later reflected in *Cancer Ward*.) He begins work on *The First Circle*.

1956   February: At the Twentieth Congress of the Communist
Party of the Soviet Union (CPSU), Nikita Khrushchev
delivers a sensational speech denouncing Stalin's crimes,
setting in motion the partial (and short-lived) liberalization of
the Soviet system that would be known as the "Thaw."

April: Solzhenitsyn's sentence of "perpetual exile" is
annulled. He moves back to European Russia at the end of
the school year and takes a position as teacher in a tiny
village east of Moscow. Life here is described in "Matryona's
Home." He continues to write in secret.

1957   February: Solzhenitsyn is officially "rehabilitated," that is, the
1945 charges against him are annulled. He remarries Natalia
Reshetovskaya (who had filed for divorce in 1949) and in
June moves to Ryazan, where he begins teaching in a local
secondary school.

1957–62   Solzhenitsyn's clandestine writing activities continue, as does
his teaching in Ryazan. He undertakes further work on *The
First Circle*, lays early plans for *The Gulag Archipelago*, and
completes *One Day in the Life of Ivan Denisovich* and
"Matryona's Home."

1961   October: The Twenty-Second Congress of the CPSU is the
high-water mark in Khrushchev's campaign to discredit
Stalin's legacy and it becomes an important factor in
Solzhenitsyn's decision to risk submitting the manuscript of
One Day to *Novy Mir*, the Soviet Union's most prestigious
literary monthly.

1962   November: The appearance of *One Day* in *Novy Mir* is met
with virtually universal acclaim in the official Soviet press.
Solzhenitsyn is inducted into the Union of Soviet Writers.

1963–64   The enthusiastic official approval of *One Day* begins to wane
rapidly. The work does not win the Lenin Prize as many had
hoped. *The First Circle* is denied publication, and negative

criticism on the writer appears with increasing frequency in the Soviet press. Solzhenitsyn begins work on *Cancer Ward*. An avalanche of letters from former zeks in response to *One Day* leads to meetings and further correspondence that provides a mass of factual material for *The Gulag Archipelago* (written in spurts between 1964 and 1968).

1964 October: Nikita Khrushchev is ousted from power in a coup headed by Leonid Brezhnev. The new regime seems intent on extirpating all vestiges of Khrushchev's "Thaw," and tightening the ideological reins on culture.

1965 A KGB raid on the apartment of Solzhenitsyn's friend results in the confiscation of a large cache of the writer's manuscripts and notes kept there.

1966 Solzhenitsyn completes *Cancer Ward*, but publication of the work in the Soviet Union is stalled. He becomes increasingly combative in his protests and public statements, regularly using the samizdat network to air his views. This typically leads to the publication of his statements abroad and to their subsequent return to the USSR via Radio Liberty.

1968 *The First Circle* and *Cancer Ward* are published abroad both in Russian and in translation. *The Gulag Archipelago* is completed, and a microfilm of this work is spirited to the West.

1969 Solzhenitsyn works intensively on *August 1914*. (The first edition is published in Paris in 1971.) He is expelled from the Writers' Union.

1970 Solzhenitsyn is awarded the Nobel Prize for Literature "for the ethical force with which he has pursued the indispensable traditions of Russian literature."

1971 August: The KGB's attempt to assassinate Solzhenitsyn fails but causes an acute illness lasting two months which the writer does not link to foul play at the time.

1971–72 Libraries across the Soviet Union are instructed to withdraw and destroy their copies of *One Day*, together with issues of *Novy Mir* containing this and other works by Solzhenitsyn.

1973 Spring: Solzhenitsyn divorces Reshetovskaya after several years of estrangement and marries Natalia Svetlova.

August: The KGB discovers a copy of *The Gulag Archipelago* typescript, whereupon Solzhenitsyn gives the signal for the work to be published abroad. The first volume appears in Paris at the end of December, making front-page news in the West.

1974 February 12: After an intense campaign of vilification in the Soviet media, Solzhenitsyn is arrested, charged with treason, stripped of his Soviet citizenship, and deported to West Germany. His family is permitted to join him later.

1974–76 Solzhenitsyn first settles in Zurich, Switzerland, moving to Cavendish, Vermont in mid-1976. Numerous public appearances mark the writer's first several years abroad.

1977 The Russian Memorial Library, a repository of unpublished materials bearing on twentieth-century Russian history, is established. An appeal in émigré newspapers yields a huge number of manuscripts, and during the following decade, about a dozen volumes of memoirs drawn from these materials are published in a series sponsored by Solzhenitsyn.

1978 The Russian-language *Collected Works* (*Sobranie sochinenii*) is launched under the writer's direct supervision. It eventually encompasses twenty volumes, including the entire ten-volume *Red Wheel* cycle: *August 1914*, 2 vols. (2d ed., 1983); *October 1916*, 2 vols. (1984); *March 1917*, 4 vols. (1986–87); and *April 1917*, 2 vols. (1991).

1989 Solzhenitsyn's works are published in the Soviet Union for the first time since the 1960s.

1990 Solzhenitsyn's Soviet citizenship is restored.

1990–91   A number of Solzhenitsyn's works, including *The First Circle*, *The Gulag Archipelago*, and *The Red Wheel* cycle are serialized in major Soviet journals.

1991   August: An attempted coup by Soviet hard-liners fails, leading to a collapse of the entire Soviet regime and a disintegration of the U.S.S.R. into its constituent republics.

    September: The charge of treason leveled against Solzhenitsyn in 1974 is officially annulled, clearing the formal barrier to his return to Russia.

1994   May: Solzhenitsyn returns to Russia via Siberia and settles in a Moscow suburb.

1994–95   The writer makes regular appearances on Russian television. His access to air time is abruptly canceled in October, 1995.

1996   The Russian Memorial Library collection is shipped to Moscow.

II  CRITICISM

The Mask of Solzhenitsyn:
Ivan Denisovich

ROBERT LOUIS JACKSON

The narrator in Solzhenitsyn's "Matryona's Home" (1963) reconciles himself to his meager diet in Matryona's house because, as he puts it, "life had taught me not to find the meaning of everyday life in food." With this statement Solzhenitsyn's narrator illuminates an ancient truth: "Man lives not by bread alone."[1] In *One Day in the Life of Ivan Denisovich* (1962), however, Solzhenitsyn's hero, Ivan Denisovich Shukhov, seems to find the meaning of life in food, clothes, and other everyday necessities. For Shukhov, food is life itself. His bowl of soup is like "rain in time of drought" (136; *91*).[2] When he puts on a warm pair of boots, "life [is] a bed of roses" (12; *13*). There is a direct connection between body and spirit.

Shukhov puts all his physical and mental energies into the struggle for survival. Yet, paradoxically, in his struggle for bread and boots he rises above the level of the material; he does not lose his self-respect and dignity, but gains them. In the final analysis, he becomes an embodiment of a wisdom that is instructive beyond the boundaries of the Gulag. Shukhov, in Solzhenitsyn's conception, gives expression to a life principle that is at once beyond good and evil and generative of ethical values. In this respect, he bears a certain resemblance (despite considerable differences in personality) to Platon Karataev in *War and Peace*. Yet, like Tolstoy's hero, the integral and well-adjusted Shukhov has his problematic side. For all his energy and resourcefulness, Shukhov has not yet emerged as a fully self-conscious and socially aware individual. His naive, childlike quality is not simply an authorial device; it is a social statement. With the appearance of *One Day*, Aleksandr Tvardovsky wrote, in his preface to that work in 1962, "a new, original, and mature talent" was born. But the face of the author of *One Day* was veiled. Unlike Dostoevsky, who in *Notes from the House of the Dead* (1860–62) chose a narrator of his own class, background, and education to mediate the impressions and experiences of his years in prison, Solzhenitsyn used the device of omniscient narrator and selected a simple, uneducated peasant-convict as the main focus of his narrative. Solzhenitsyn, of course, does not cede his higher perception to the average Shukhov; like Tolstoy, he expresses his most vital thoughts not only through occasional comments but through the juxtaposition of materials, the subtle configuration and interaction of character and situation. Yet it is Shukhov, his activities, his interests, his moods that set the general tone of *One Day*. We experience the Gulag as Shukhov experiences it.

In the series of memorable writings that followed *One Day* – Solzhenitsyn's first published work – the author makes his way to the foreground.[3] In *Gulag Archipelago* he steps out onto the stage and speaks in his own voice, "on behalf of those who have perished." "Everything *will be told*," he writes in a terse preface. The story is told in a voice hoarse with rage, bitterness, and impatience. Impatience with lying, impatience with inertia, impatience with patience. We recognize in the narrator of this "experiment in literary investigation" a descendant of Pavel Ivanych in Chekhov's story "Gusev" (1890), that ailing "man of uncertain social status" who, returning by ship to Russia from Siberia, "sleeps sitting up," "fears nobody and nothing," "always speaks the truth outright":

> I am embodied protest. I see despotism – I protest, I see cant and hypocrisy – I protest, I see triumphant swine – I protest. And I am invincible, no Spanish inquisition can compel me to be silent. Yes . . . Cut off my tongue – and I will protest in mimicry; wall me up in a cellar – I will cry out from there in a manner that will be heard a mile beyond. . . . All my acquaintances say to me: "You are a most unbearable person, Pavel Ivanych!" I am proud of such a reputation. . . . My friends write from Russia: "Don't come."

But here I am going back to spite them . . . Yes . . . Now that's life as I understand it.[4]

The writer who would shortly provoke the wrath of Soviet authorities is hidden in *One Day*. The reader, of course, has no difficulty sensing Solzhenitsyn's pain and bitterness in this work; he does not mistake the curiously well-adjusted Shukhov for the author, though he may at first be puzzled by the latter's emphasis on Shukhov's art of adaptation as opposed to what might have been a more satisfying picture (for the militant reader) of an attitude of defiance, withdrawal, or self-destruction. But Shukhov is not a dissident. As Tvardovsky rightly remarks in his preface to *One Day*: The pain and bitterness we find there do not convey a feeling of "utter despair."[5] Indeed, we find in *One Day* the organic and epic affirmation of a Leo Tolstoy. What Tvardovsky further calls "a picture of exceptional vividness and truthfulness about the nature of man"[6] owes almost everything to Solzhenitsyn's characterization of the integral, energetic, above all patient and enduring nature of Ivan Denisovich Shukhov.

"Yes, man has vitality!" (*Da, chelovek zhivuch!*) exclaims the narrator of Dostoevsky's *House of the Dead* as he contemplates the life of the convicts in their prison hell. "Man is a creature who adapts to everything, and that is the best way of defining him." Adaptation here is not only negative, pointing only to man's readiness to compromise his humanity, but it is also positive in character: man adapts to a difficult, dangerous, and often terrifying environment in order to survive. In adapting, however, he discloses his vitality, his strength, his will to live; in adapting he learns to master his environment, and in turn he shapes himself. The behavior of the convicts in the prisons of both Dostoevsky and Solzhenitsyn attests to their inability fully to submit to the killing routine of prison life, to a dehumanizing environment, to a world without exit. Solzhenitsyn nonetheless approaches the prison experience quite differently than does Dostoevsky.

The great nineteenth-century novelist takes the reader on a journey through the kaleidoscopic world of prison life. The narrator of *House of the Dead* eschews a "systematic and orderly" description of his ten years in prison. "Such a description," he observes, "would of necessity become very monotonous. All the happenings would have too much of the same coloring." Instead, Dostoevsky's narrator presents in "one clear and vivid picture" a colorful panorama of life in prison with its work routines, its religious holidays, its theatricals, its punishments, its attempted escapes, prison folklore and songs, and so on. We see the convicts in the calm and reconciling hindsight of an educated ex-convict who has left prison. This same ex-convict, the narrator, expatiates on the great themes of human nature: freedom, fate, responsibility, evil, crime and punishment. The setting and treatment of the prison world are epic.[7]

The task Solzhenitsyn set himself was at once both more limited and, from an artistic point of view, more difficult. He chooses *one* ordinary day in the life of an ordinary Russian convict. He forgoes a description of exceptional individuals and types, extraordinary incidents and cruelties that were to be found in the typical Gulag environment. Rather, he concentrates on the killing monotony and routine of prison life, the convict's constant confrontation and coping with the brutal yet ordinary, often uninteresting but always vital necessities of existence. In short, Solzhenitsyn risks a narrative in which all the happenings have "too much of the same coloring."

Dostoevsky's narrator leads the reader into prison and out of it. The movement in the *House of the Dead* is from winter to spring, Christmas to Easter, death to resurrection. The reader watches as the narrator's fetters are struck off, and he hears him exclaim in the last line of the work: "Freedom, a new life, resurrection from the dead . . . What a glorious moment!" The reader knows that other people remain in prison, perhaps forever, but he or she feels liberated at the end of Dostoevsky's *House of the Dead*.

The movement in *One Day* is circular and repetitive, and leads nowhere. Shukhov is preoccupied with the same pressing concerns at all hours of the day: food, warmth, physical security, frenzied work schedules, and so on. "A convict's thoughts are no freer than he is:

they come back to the same place, worry over the same thing continually. Will they poke around in my mattress and find my bread
ration? Can I get off work if I report sick tonight?" (40; *30*). The
reader gets up in the morning at 5:00 A.M. with Shukhov and, after a
grueling day, goes to bed with him at night. The environment is
tense with everyday needs and efforts, but little that is dramatic has
"happened." For Shukhov, however, the day has been eventful.

> Shukhov felt pleased with life as he went to sleep. A lot of good
> things had happened that day. He hadn't been thrown in the hole.
> The gang hadn't been dragged off to Sotsgorodok. He'd swiped
> the extra gruel at dinnertime. The foreman had got a good rate
> for the job. He'd enjoyed working on the wall. He hadn't been
> caught with the blade at the search point. He'd earned a bit from
> Tsezar that evening. And he'd bought his tobacco. The end of an
> unclouded day. Almost a happy one. (181; *120*)

Shukhov's fetters, however, are not struck off at this point. And
the reader grasps the irony of Shukhov's contentment. Solzhenitsyn's
last words are like nails driven into a coffin. "Just one of the 3,653
days of his sentence, from bell to bell. The extra three were for leap
years" (182; *120*).

One student of Solzhenitsyn has commented that the "weight of
the entire novel is balanced against these last lines, as though Shukhov tries everything within his powers to fend off this idea, but
finally, just before unconsciousness, at the margin of his self, the idea
forces its way out, the idea of freedom. Despite everything, despite
all his adjustments and skills and victories, he wants to be free,
simply that. Nothing more. Free."[8] It is Solzhenitsyn, however, not
Shukhov, who utters the last words in the novel. (Not without reason
are the last lines of *One Day* set off from the rest of the text.) And
here is the deeper tragic content of *One Day*: For all his misery and
his indubitable desire to get out of prison, the Russian peasant, as
Solzhenitsyn depicts him in Shukhov, does not grasp the full enor-
mity of his situation in prison or in Russian life. He is lost in the
chaos of Russian life and history. In this respect, Shukhov's adjust-

ments and skills, his remarkable powers of adaptation, while wholly admirable from one point of view, nonetheless reflect a certain fatalism. "We want him to scream a little more," the same student of Solzhenitsyn complains apropos of Shukhov's feeling that nobody owed him a living. "And that, again, is why those last lines . . . are so important. They remind us that inside the well-adjusted Shukhov, from whom we are meant to learn so much, there is another man, not at all well-adjusted, from whom we can learn nothing."[9] Here, perhaps, we are involved in wishful thinking. In *One Day* Solzhenitsyn brings us to the brink of one of the most difficult and painful questions in Russian life: How does the average Russian man orient to his historical fate? What is particularly striking about Solzhenitsyn's treatment of the Russian peasant Shukhov in *One Day* is precisely that he does not posit another maladjusted man in the depths of Shukhov. As we have suggested, Solzhenitsyn does not scream in *One Day*. One might surmise, perhaps, that he screams in his other major works because the Russian man is too well-adjusted to his fate.

Time moves rapidly in prison, but leads nowhere. Shukhov was always struck by "how time flew when you were working. He'd often noticed that days in the camp rolled by before you knew it. Yet your sentence stood still, the time you had to serve never got any less" (67; 47). The endless time, however, is filled with countless petty detail and marked by a relentless struggle for survival. Shukhov "never overslept. He was always up at the call. That way he had an hour and a half all to himself before work parade – time for a man who knew his way around to earn a bit on the side." But there were always many other people with the same idea. "It's the law of the taiga here, men," one convict remarks. "But a man *can* live here, just like anywhere else" (4; 7). But to live, one must be alert at every moment, active and attentive to the most minute details of day-to-day life. Details are the bane of Shukhov's life, but details, even infinitesimal ones, are also the source of extraordinary satisfactions: a long-awaited draw on a cigarette butt, the discovery of a useful piece of steel, sucking on a fish bone, or the enjoyment of a pair of boots. Shukhov's pleasure in a pair of sturdy boots can only be compared with Akaky Akakievich's pleasure in his new overcoat in Gogol's story "The Overcoat": "He'd walked around for a whole week as though it was his birthday, making a clatter with his new heels. Then, in December, felt boots had turned up as well: Life was a bed of roses, no need to die just yet" (12–13; *13*). Shukhov, however, had to turn in his old boots: a prisoner was not allowed to have two pairs at a time. "He'd never missed anything so much in all those eight years" (Ibid.).

Nowhere do tiny satisfactions attain such major proportions as in the realm of eating. For the half-starved Shukhov, as for the other convicts, even the meager rations are a feast. These momentary pleasures are experienced slowly in the midst of haste.

> [Pavlo] picked up Shukhov's portion of bread from the table and held it out. A little hillock of sugar had been scooped onto it. Shukhov was in a great hurry, but still thanked him properly. . . . Nor was he in too much of a hurry to dip his lips in the sugar and lick them, as he hoisted himself up with one foot on the bed bracket to straighten his bedding, or to view his bread ration from all angles and weigh it on his hand in mid-air, wondering whether it contained the regulation five hundred and fifty grams. (25; *21*)

Or again:

> Taking it for granted that one of the bowls he'd swiped would be his, Shukhov quickly set about the one he'd earned by the sweat of his brow. . . . This minute should have been devoted solely to the business of eating – spooning the thin layer of gruel from the bottom of the bowl, cautiously raising it to his mouth, and rolling it around with his tongue. But he had to hurry, so that Pavlo would see him finish and offer him the second portion. (80; *55–56*).

Economy of material, economy of energy, economy of time define Shukhov's entire approach to prison life. He is patient, but not passive. He approaches his prison environment like Robinson Crusoe: with endless enterprise. Nothing is neglected. He stitches "covers for somebody's mittens from a piece of old lining" (3; 7) in exchange for something; he picks up bowls from the table and takes piles of them to the dishwasher in order to get a bit of food; he makes his own spoon out of a piece of wire and keeps it in his boot; he pockets a bit of steel broken off a hacksaw blade lying in the snow ("you never knew what you might need later" [86; 60]); he carefully sews a piece of bread into his mattress for later on; and, during a meal, he saves a crust of bread to clean out the mush in his bowl. Survival involves such diverse details as warming your feet properly by the stove before going off to work, doffing your hat to a guard, and avoiding clashes with those in authority. "You had to be wide awake all the time" – or they'd be on top of you (19; 17). In his life Shukhov strikes a balance between the aggressiveness needed to survive and the compromises needed to live. You had to get your ration of bread. Your life depended on it. "Your life can depend on those two hundred grams" (63; 45). But at the same time you had to understand and obey the unwritten laws and mores of prison life. Survival always depended on a certain respect for the needs of others, in particular your own work group.

In the *House of the Dead*, Dostoevsky speaks of the smuggler as a "poet in part." "He risks everything, runs terrible dangers, dissembles, invents, dodges, wriggles out of difficult situations." Shukhov, like the smuggler, is a kind of Odysseus of prison life, a man – to borrow Homer's words – of "many turns," "adept in all kinds of devices and toil." In Shukhov, as in Odysseus, there is an inherent ambiguity. Intelligence in him takes the form of both wisdom and cunning.

The down-to-earth, embodied wisdom of Shukhov recalls Thoreau. In *Walden*, the American philosopher observes:

It would be some advantage to live a primitive and frontier life . . . if only to learn what are the gross necessaries of life and what methods have been taken to obtain them. . . . By *necessary of life*, I mean whatever, of all that man obtains by his own exertions, has been from the first, or from long use has become so important to human life that few, if any . . . ever attempt to do without it. To many creatures there is in this sense but one necessary of life, Food. . . .The necessaries of life for man in this climate . . . [are] Food, Shelter, Clothing, and Fuel.[10]

With respect to his own experiment, Thoreau remarks:

> I went to the woods because I wished to live deliberately, to front only the essential facts of life, and see if I could learn what it had to teach, and not, when I came to die, discover that I had not lived. I did not wish to live what was not life, living is so dear; nor did I wish to practice resignation, unless it was quite necessary. I wanted to live so sturdily and Spartan-like as to put to rout all that was not life, to cut a broad swath and shave close, to drive life into a corner, and reduce it to its lowest terms.[11]

One cannot say that even a fragment of Thoreau's speculations enter, or could enter, Shukhov's head. The last thing one could say about him was that he sought to conduct an experiment with life, to set about reducing life to "its lowest terms." Shukhov is neither a philosopher nor an outsider. He certainly does not choose to live in the Gulag. His life here is enforced economy and restriction of the most terrible kind. And yet compelled to confront what Thoreau in the freedom of his experiment called the "necessaries of life" – what man obtains through his own exertions – Shukhov not only overcomes the determinism of his prison existence, but quite unconsciously exemplifies those values of simplicity, a direct and organic relationship to life that Thoreau highlights in *Walden* and that Tolstoy idealizes in the half-mythic figure of Platon Karataev in *War and Peace*. "To affect the quality of the day," remarks Thoreau, "that is the highest of arts."[12] It was Solzhenitsyn's great achievement in *One Day in the Life of Ivan Denisovich* to demonstrate that the simple Russian peasant Shukhov, in the most extreme conditions, is a great artist when it comes to affecting "the quality of the day." Yet Shukhov's motivating impulse is neither aesthetic nor didactic; of the most organic sort, it reduces itself to one thought: survival. "We shall survive. We shall survive it all. God willing, we'll see the end of it!" (153; *101*).

Gulag, as it is experienced by Shukhov, is a melting down in which the oldest instincts of personality are brought into full play. Here, first of all, is the energy, cunning, and vitality that comes from confronting danger and a world where the issues are, quite simply, life and death. "No need to die just yet" (12–13; *13*). Yet though this is a "taiga" where it is every man for himself, Shukhov manages to retain a basic dignity and decency. He responds to kindness and is capable of doing a good deed for others (giving another person a smoke, a cookie, etc.). Yet the good that we perceive in him is not the result of some conscious moral principle or religious persuasion. He does not experience pity or compassion in the Dostoevskian mode. Dostoevsky signaled his Christian ideal in the figure of the handsome Dagestan Tatar Aley. It is this nearly Christlike figure who gives expression to Dostoevsky's highest values of love and forgiveness. Solzhenitsyn's respectful distance in *One Day* from a conventional Christian outlook is reflected in Shukhov's conversation with the Baptist Alyoshka at the end of the novel. Alyoshka counsels Shukhov not to pray for his freedom:

> What good is freedom to you? If you're free, your faith will soon be choked by thorns! Be glad you're in prison. Here you have time to think about your soul. Remember what the Apostle Paul says, 'What are you doing, weeping and breaking my heart? For I am ready not only to be imprisoned but even to die in Jerusalem for the name of the Lord Jesus.'" (177–78; *117*)[13]

Alyoshka's remarks perhaps echo moments of bitterness and pessimism that Solzhenitsyn experienced in his own years of imprisonment. Shukhov's response to Alyoshka suggests how near the brink of despair a convict can stand:

> Shukhov stared at the ceiling and said nothing. He no longer knew whether he wanted to be free or not. To begin with, he'd wanted it very much, and counted up every evening how many

days he still had to serve. Then he'd got fed up with it. And still later it had gradually dawned on him that people like himself were not allowed to go home but were packed off into exile. And there was no knowing where the living was easier – here or there. The one thing he might want to ask God for was to let him go home. But *they* wouldn't let him go home. (178; *117–18*)

In the end Shukhov, like Solzhenitsyn, rejects the path of conventional Christian resignation. Look, Shukhov says to Alyoshka, "it's worked out pretty well for you. Christ told you to go to jail, and you did it, for Christ. But what am I here for? Because they weren't ready for the war in '41 – is that the reason? Was that my fault?" (178; *118*).

It would be a mistake to confuse the naive, half-pagan Shukhov with Solzhenitsyn in this conversation with Alyoshka the Baptist. Yet the blunt and down-to-earth Shukhov would certainly seem to reflect certain aspects of Solzhenitsyn's personality and even of his approach to the virtues of Christian humility. The humble, loving Jesus does not seem to have been a model for Solzhenitsyn as he was for Dostoevsky.[14] The great Russian writer of the Soviet period sometimes seems closer to Judaism than to Christianity in his deep preoccupation with justice, in his nationalism, and, finally, in his proud conception of himself as prophet and avenger. Solzhenitsyn comes not as a messenger of the humble Jesus, but as the emissary of the vindictive God of the Old Testament. If the spirit of Solzhenitsyn is reflected in any single character in *One Day*, it is probably in the "tall old man" who was "straightbacked as could be" (154; *102*), whose face looked as if it were "dark chiseled stone," and who in all his years in the Gulag "refused to knuckle under" (155; *103*). The old man is silent. What is he thinking? Solzhenitsyn does not tell us, but the demeanor of this man, we may guess, suggests a mood found in the 137th Psalm:

> If I forget thee, O Jerusalem, let my right hand forget her cunning.
> If I do not remember thee, let my tongue cleave to the roof

of my mouth; if I prefer not Jerusalem above my chief joy.

Remember, O Lord, the children of Edom in the day of
Jerusalem; who said, Rase it, rase it, even to the founda-
tion thereof.

O daughter of Babylon, who art to be destroyed; happy shall
he be, that rewardeth thee as thou hast served us.

Happy shall he be, that taketh and dasheth thy little ones
against the stones.

This Solzhenitsyn was not revealed in *One Day*. But flashes of
lightning were already visible on the horizon.

NOTES

An earlier version of this article was published in German translation:
"Solshenizyn. *Ein Tag im Leben des Iwan Denissowitsch,*" in *Die Russishe Nov-
elle,* ed. Bodo Zelinsky (Düsseldorf: Bagel, 1982), pp. 242–51. Copyright ©
by Robert L. Jackson. Reprinted by permission.

1. For a discussion of this story, see Robert Louis Jackson, "'Matryona's
Home': The Making of a Russian Icon," in Kathryn Feuer, ed., *Solzhenitsyn:
A Collection of Critical Essays* (Englewood Cliffs, N.J.: Prentice-Hall, 1976),
pp. 60–70.

2. The parenthetical page references are, respectively, to the H. T. Willetts translation of *One Day in the Life of Ivan Denisovich* (New York: Noon-
day; Farrar Straus Giroux, 1991), and to the Russian original as published in
Aleksandr Solzhenitsyn, *Sobranie sochinenii,* vol. 3 (Vermont and Paris:
YMCA Press, 1978). The page reference to the Russian text is given in
italics.

3. It should be noted that for a number of years before he published *One
Day,* Solzhenitsyn had been composing various works "for the drawer." *The
First Circle* (finished in 1958), for example, definitely preceded the writing of
One Day, though it appeared outside Russia only in 1968, that is, well after
the publication of *One Day.*

4. I should mention in passing that figures of almost dogmatic and trucu-
lent independence such as Pavel Ivanych for the most part were *not* depicted
in a positive light in nineteenth-century Russian literature. Pavel Ivanych,
for all the "truth" that he embodies, is a reincarnation of Dostoevsky's

Underground Man and as such is an ambiguous figure. Indeed Chekhov approaches Pavel Ivanych very critically. Yet this not totally unsympathetic portrait of a protestor in a culture that was hostile to radical individualism remains striking. On this matter, see my article, "Bibleiskie i literaturnye alliuzii v rasskaze 'Gusev' (Biblical and literary allusions in 'Gusev')" in V. B. Kataev, R.-D. Kluge, and R. Norhejl, eds., *Anton P. Čechov: Philosophie und Religion in Leben und Werk* (Munich: Kubon & Sagner, 1997), pp. 419–26.

5. Aleksandr Tvardovskii, "Vmesto predisloviia," *Novyi mir*, 1962, no. 11, p. 9.

6. Ibid.

7. For a full discussion of these questions in Dostoevsky's *Notes from the House of the Dead*, see Robert Louis Jackson, *The Art of Dostoevsky: Deliriums and Nocturnes* (Princeton, N.J.: Princeton University Press, 1981), pp. 33–169.

8. Steven Allaback, *Alexander Solzhenitsyn* (New York: Taplinger, 1978), p. 54.

9. Ibid., p. 57.

10. Henry David Thoreau, *Walden*, in *The Portable Thoreau* (New York: Viking, 1947), p. 267.

11. Ibid., pp. 343–44.

12. Ibid., p. 343.

13. Acts 21:13.

14. For a view of Solzhenitsyn as a "Christian writer," one based on the writer's "intuition of creation, fall, and redemption," see Alexander Schmemann's essay, "On Solzhenitsyn," in John B. Dunlop, Richard Haugh, and Alexis Klimoff, eds., *Aleksandr Solzhenitsyn: Critical Essays and Documentary Materials*, 2d ed. (New York: Collier, 1975), pp. 33–44. Schmemann's definition of a Christian writer is of course unusually broad. Many writers would qualify as Christian writers under this definition.

The Geometry of Hell: The Poetics of Space and Time in *One Day in the Life of Ivan Denisovich*

RICHARD TEMPEST

Many of Solzhenitsyn's fictions are set within an enclosed, artificially constructed space – a prison, a peasant hut, a labor camp, a hospital – with its own topography, its own history, and occasionally its own flora and fauna. Each of these self-contained worlds is inhabited by a group of people, a little mankind with its own social hierarchies and personal relationships. The characters in *One Day in the Life of Ivan Denisovich*, *The First Circle*, and *Cancer Ward* suffer, feel, move, work, converse, argue, reminisce, and meditate within these cubic, parallelepipedal, prismatic, cylindrical – but always geometrically regular – spaces. Their lives are physically constricted and conditioned by space, which is a function of such constants of the human condition as loneliness, poverty, disease, prison.

Beyond the constricted and constricting space inhabited by Solzhenitsyn's characters there lies another space, like the village of Torfoprodukt in "Matryona's Home," the city of Moscow in *The First Circle*, or the city of Tashkent in *Cancer Ward*. The dramatic unity of closed space is disrupted when the narration forays into this external, more open territory. The dichotomy of closed space/open space always corresponds to important oppositions within Solzhenitsyn's fictive world: the lie versus the truth, corruption versus honesty, sickness versus health, unfreedom versus freedom. The prisoners in *One Day* have no access to the world outside the camp. The city, the village, the countryside is to them but a memory, one that for Ivan Shukhov, for example, has the quality of a dream.

The events described in *One Day* occur within several sets of closed space: the Special Camp, the building site, and the spaces-within-a-space they contain – the barracks, sick bay, mess hut, auto-repair shop. Only when the column of prisoners marches to and from the building site does the narration function within an open, unbordered, unmarked area. Yet even here the prisoners follow an ordained route (it runs in a *straight* line) to which they must cleave – quite literally, on pain of death.[1]

The hierarchies and relationships among the inhabitants of the Special Camp constitute a kind of fourth dimension, in addition to the three geometrical dimensions of closed space within which the action unfolds. I use the term *dimension* advisedly, for there is a unity of style, imagery, and artistic intent between Solzhenitsyn's description of the social structure of camp society and his sustained emphasis on the geometrical structure of the camp itself. The characters in *One Day* inhabit not only a particular geographical and geometrical space, but also a special kind of social space.

The "geometrical" quality of Solzhenitsyn's works was remarked on by none other than the author himself. In a 1966 interview he stated, "Approached by art, every individual phenomenon becomes a 'bundle of intersecting planes,' to use a mathematical analogy: several planes of reality are unexpectedly seen to intersect at the chosen point."[2]

Tinker, tailor, soldier, sailor, rich man, poor man, beggarman, thief – the entire gallery of social types listed in the nursery rhyme is to be found inside this patch of steppe cordoned off by barbed wire. Camp society is intensely hierarchical: it is, to use a term from anthropology, *ranked*. At the bottom are the scavengers like Fetyukov, the lowliest of the low, who have been reduced to licking the bowls in the camp canteen. They are the camp's marginals, and their fate is death. Then come the prisoners who have been assigned to general duties – heavy manual labor on building sites outside the camp compound. These men, who are grouped into work gangs, form the majority of the camp population. Then come the deputy foremen and the foremen, and then the trustees, inmates who perform various chores within the camp: the cooks, hairdressers, artists, and medical personnel. Then come the hated informers and stooges like the brutal Der or the barrack orderly, a professional criminal who "isn't afraid of anybody, because he's got the camp brass behind him" (168; *111*). Then come the warders and guards. And, finally, at the apex of this social pyramid stands the camp commandant, a sinister, remote and mysterious figure whose name we never learn.

The Special Camp may be seen as a dark parody of the ideal state, Callipolis, described by Plato in the *Republic*. The Greek philosopher divided the population of his utopia into three hereditary classes: the guardians, who rule; the auxiliary class, who police and fight on their behalf; and the laborers, who are the most numerous and least privileged group. These Platonic parallels may be extended further. What art exists in the Special Camp has, like art in Plato's Callipolis, been harnessed to the service of the state: the murals in the free workers' recreation center, presumably painted by the three captive artists in the camp, are, we surmise, examples of Socialist Realist kitsch, propaganda exhorting the toiling masses to ever greater heights of industrial productivity.[3] The three artists also draw the prisoners' identity numbers (another *useful* activity) and, working on the side, supply the bosses with what one imagines are suitably flattering portraits of them and their families or pretty landscapes to soothe their authoritarian eyes.

The chances of survival for the individual prisoner are directly related to the type of space he works in. The ordinary zeks labor *outside*, in the open steppe, where they must not only exert themselves physically but must also cope with the elements: "The wind whistles over the bare steppe – hot and dry in summer, freezing in winter" (75; *52*). The trusties are assigned to light duties which they perform *inside* buildings that are heated and relatively comfortable, like the parcel room or the mess hut.

In addition to the all-important hierarchy of camp status or caste, there are other hierarchies in this little mankind, which are based on the numerous differences among the inmates: differences of age,

prison experience, character, nationality, profession, religion, education, political belief, wealth, health.

There is yet another, fictive, dimension to the world described in
the story. Like Solzhenitsyn's other works, *One Day* presents a mosaic
of individual chronicles – the biographical dossiers of the major and
minor characters, which are invariably placed within the context of
the epic and tragic events of twentieth-century Russian history. Always these chronicles are centered around the political sins of omis-
sion or commission, of thought or deed, of parentage or association,
that led to the arrest and imprisonment of the individual "sinner."

In the preface to *The Gulag Archipelago* Solzhenitsyn describes the
Soviet camp system as an "amazing country . . . an almost invisible,
almost imperceptible country inhabited by the zek people."[4] Like his
three-volume "literary investigation" of that strange and terrible
country, *One Day* was meant to make the invisible visible, the imperceptible perceptible, and the prisoners, anonymous in their huddled
masses, identifiable as living and suffering human beings.

The impact of *One Day* on Soviet readers was such that on the
strength of this work alone its author, an obscure provincial schoolteacher, was declared by many to be a second Tolstoy. This is how a
contemporary described the experience of reading Solzhenitsyn's
story for the first time:

> I felt I was gradually being transported to another world. Yet
> the manner in which I was being transported there was unlike the
> manner in which one willingly immerses oneself in a world of
> pleasurable impressions or the manner in which strong impres-
> sions intrude into one's own world and fill it. I entered this differ-
> ent world on my own, slowly and with difficulty, forcing my way
> through the stylistic structure and the unfamiliar language forms,
> cutting through the spiritual fabric that separated our worlds,
> which was twined by barbed wire and covered with icy growths,
> overcoming the shock and bemusement caused by the strangeness
> of this world, of its inhabitants, their thoughts and deeds, their life
> (their *non-life!*) . . . This was so hard that after a while I was

physically unable to continue. I raised my eyes from the book and looked around: here I too was surrounded by people and lights – not by the camp compound with prisoners scurrying across it, but by the well-lit reading room with its calm and thoughtful readers. I was unable to remain in place and left the room. . . . Again I immersed myself in the book and again after a while I had to interrupt my reading in order to regain my breath. This happened several times.[5]

This reader (or, to use a modern critical term, *receptor*) experienced the state that in his *Biographia Literaria* Coleridge famously described as the "willing suspension of disbelief": the state of receptivity and credulity in which a person reading a literary work is prepared to recognize the reality of the characters, events, and settings described in it. Yet so powerful was the impact of Solzhenitsyn's story on this individual that his very suspension of disbelief was too painful for him to endure, even though (or perhaps because) he had ensconced himself in an institutional environment – that of a library reading room – expressly designed to facilitate the evolvement of that mental state in a reader.

Such a trans-literary experience is akin to the impact on a religious believer of an artistic depiction of the Apocalypse or of Hell. If the Soviet Union, in the words of the famous patriotic song of 1935, was a secular paradise where "man never breathed so freely," in *One Day in the Life of Ivan Denisovich* it is shown as the kind of place where every breath may be one's last.

Now Hell is a frequent image, metaphor, and theme in both Western and Russian literature: "Hell hath no limits . . . where we are is Hell" (Marlowe); "My self am Hell" (Milton); "Hell is a city much like London" (Shelley); "Hell is oneself" (T. S. Eliot); "Hell, it's other people" (Sartre). Wuthering Heights in Emily Brontë's eponymous novel is a Satanic household; the referent for this work was Milton's *Paradise Lost*. In Nikolai Gogol's *Dead Souls* the entire land of Russia is depicted as a kind of grey inferno, where the traveling salesman Chichikov barters for titles of ownership to the souls of dead peasants with a succession of bestial and even demonic landowners. Gogol was inspired by the *Divine Comedy*; his epic was the first part of a projected trilogy that was meant to describe Russia as hell, purgatory, and paradise. Solzhenitsyn's novel *The First Circle* contains a plethora of allusions to Dante's famous poem, starting with the title, although here Hell is present as a transmuted, literary image in which the religious element is subsumed by the artistic one.

If the secret laboratory with its staff of captive scientists in Solzhenitsyn's novel is the first circle of this Soviet hell, the Special Camp is one of its lower rings – though not the lowest, for there existed even more terrible places in the Gulag, like the camps described by Varlam Shalamov in his *Kolyma Tales* (or the camp in Ust-Izhma, where Ivan Denisovich spent the first years of his prison sentence).

Of the many torments that the political "sinners" in the Special Camp must endure the chief one is trial by cold. Ice and snow, of course, are a prominent element in traditional descriptions of Hell. The *Apocalypse of Paul*, an early Christian text dating from Roman times, shows the damned suffering not only in pits of fire but also in pits of snow. In the *Vision of Tundal* (1149) the eponymous hero, an Irish knight who visits Hell, sees "a mountain with fire on one side, ice and snow on the other, and hailstorms in between."[6] Another twelfth-century work, *The Elucidarium*, lists nine kinds of tortures inflicted on the damned, one of which is torture by unbearable cold. Works such as these formed the tradition that influenced Dante and later Milton, whose descriptions of Hell are among the most famous and enduring in Western literature.

The Special Camp in the icy steppes of Kazakhstan calls to mind the outer reaches of Milton's Hell, which are described in Book II of *Paradise Lost*. Beyond the four infernal rivers of Styx, Acheron, Cocytus, and Phlegethon, on the other side of Lethe, the river of oblivion,

> A frozen Continent
> Lies dark and wilde, beat with perpetual storms

> Of Whirlwind and dire Hail, which on firm land
> Thaws not, but gathers heap, and ruin seems
> Of ancient pile; all else deep snow and ice.[7]

In Milton's vision of Hell the damned undergo torture alternatively by flames and ice, and "cold performs th'effect of Fire."

The most terrible place in the Special Camp is the punishment block: "The walls were stone, the floor cement, there were no windows at all, the stove was kept just warm enough for the ice on the wall to melt and form puddles on the floor. You slept on bare boards, got three hundred grams of bread a day, skilly only every third day" (167–68; *111*). Ten days here mean that one's health is ruined for life. Fifteen days spell death. One recalls Milton's description of the damned "starving in Ice."[8]

And yet if the Special Camp is hell, it is peculiarly a Soviet one, with all the corruptions, absurdities, and inefficiencies characteristic of the Soviet system. The bosses embezzle, the zeks pilfer – the former to get rich, the latter to survive. The workmanship, with the significant exception of the punishment block, tends to be shoddy: the prisoners, virtual slaves that they are, have no incentive to perform quality work. The construction site, with its shabby workforce, ramshackle sheds, and abandoned industrial parts is a scene familiar to anyone who ever visited the Soviet Union.

Some of the absurdities of the camp regime are intentional: they are a form of punishment. In the Special Camps, writes Solzhenitsyn in *The Gulag Archipelago*, the warders would write down the numbers of prisoners who were guilty of infractions of the rules and then demand "written explanations" – "although pens and ink were forbidden and no paper was supplied."[9] It is precisely such explanations that Tsezar and Buynovsky must provide at the end of the day, and it is precisely the same objection that the foreman Tyurin makes to the warder on their behalf (165–66; *110*).

"The nomad is constantly on the move, eats and drinks when he can, braves all weathers, is grateful for small mercies. Everything he possesses can be bundled up at a moment's notice and his food moves with him."[10] Now Shukhov and his fellow prisoners are not nomads, though they dwell in the steppe, the nomads' traditional environment. But like nomads, they are always moving, always on the go, always prepared to endure the violence of nature or man. Like a Bedouin or a Plains Indian, Shukhov can tell the hour of the day from the position of the sun. When he sets off for the building site he carries with him all the clothes he possesses, a supply of food (a bread crust he has saved from breakfast), and all the money he has, which is secreted inside the padding of his jerkin.

Shukhov's clothes are his carapace. Just as an ethnographer would describe the garb of an exotic tribe, Solzhenitsyn explains in minute detail the design and function of the layers of clothes that protect Shukhov's body and even his face. The informed reader perceives in these threadbare bits of clothing connections to Solzhenitsyn's own epic life. When we first meet the hero he is huddled up on his bunk, covered by a blanket and jacket, his feet squeezed into the sleeve of his quilted jerkin. The same prison jerkin figures in the story "Matryona's Home," where Ignatich, the author's alter ego, merely *covers* his legs with the shabby garment: "That jerkin held memories for me: it had kept me warm in the bad years."[11] That worn-out padded jacket can be seen in the famous photograph of Solzhenitsyn dressed in his prison uniform, a photo he took himself after he was released from the Special Camp in Ekibastuz; in it, we read in *The Oak and the Calf*, he would chop wood for his stove when he lived in Ryazan.[12]

One Day contains a complete cosmography of Shukhov's world. The story begins with a brief passage that "fixes" the action within the dimensions of space and time: "The hammer banged reveille on the rail outside camp HQ at five o'clock as always. Time to get up. The ragged noise was muffled by ice two fingers thick on the windows . . . Outside, it was . . . pitch-black, except for the three yellow lights visible from the window, two in the perimeter, one inside the camp" (3; 7). To reach the ears of the protagonist the clanging of the hammer must first travel across the yards of open space between the HQ hut and the barrack. Next it must penetrate the layer of ice on the barrack window. It is ice – not distance – that muffles the harsh sound.[13] The reference to the ice on the window pane is the first indication of the severity of the climate and inaugurates one of the major themes of the work – that of the cold, the snow, and the wind, which are the chief physical threats to the prisoners' health and indeed their lives.

Already the connections between space, time, temperature, and color – the four physical values that loom large in the narrative – have been established. As Ivan Shukhov goes about his daily business inside and outside the camp, space will be defined, time measured, the colors enumerated, and the effect of cold and warmth on the prisoners' bodies recorded.

When Shukhov exits the barrack we are given a broader view of the camp: "Two big searchlights from watchtowers in opposite corners crossed beams as they swept the compound. Lights were burning around the periphery, and inside the camp, dotted around in such numbers that they made the stars look dim" (9; 11). The beams are the diagonal lines joining together pairs of opposite corners within the square or rectangular territory of the camp. Three of the perimeter lights could be seen from the narrator's vantage point at the barrack window. We now realize how narrow was the field of vision afforded by that window and are given a sense of the position of Shukhov's barrack within the compound.

Shukhov is constantly on the move. In the morning and evening he walks inside the camp compound, entering and exiting various buildings (never without reason or purpose). Together with other working zeks he marches to and from the building site. At the site he warms himself in the auto-repair shop, eats in the mess hut, and lays bricks in the open air. Shukhov's progress over the course of the day adumbrates the geometry of the space inside the camp perimeter and at the work site. The reader is provided a kind of mental grid across which he can picture the hero's movements. Fences, posts, buildings, doors, windows are the grid's points of reference.

The camp is located in the barren plains of Central Kazakhstan. The chief quality of the landscape is its flatness. This flatness is emphasized by the prisoners' posture: the cold makes them cringe and huddle; they march to the work site "hands behind back, heads lowered" (39; *30*). Once the prisoners have passed the buildings they had constructed earlier they enter the open, snow-covered steppe, "walking into the wind and the reddening sunrise" (we are thus told the direction in which they are going) (40; *31*). We recall Claudio's vision of Hell in *Measure for Measure*:

> Ay, but to die, and go we know not where;
> To lie in cold obstruction and to rot;
> This sensible warm motion to become
> A kneaded clod; and the delighted spirit
> To bathe in fiery floods, or to reside
> In thrilling region of thick-ribbed ice;
> To be imprison'd in the viewless winds,
> And blown with restless violence round about
> The pendent world.[14]

By the time the column arrives at the construction site the sun has risen and we are given a panoramic view of the place: "Looking through the wire gate, across the building site and out through the wire fence on the far side, you could see the sun rising, big and red" (45; *33*). The image of the sun as seen through the strands of barbed wire is fraught with symbolism and is made all the more telling by the fact that the author leaves it to the reader to complete the picture. As our mind's eye follows three walking figures – the two guards who are making their way to their respective watchtowers (which are "distant") and the escort commander who sets off for the guard house – we acquire an idea of the size and layout of the site (45; *33*).

Occasionally the adumbration of space proceeds on a very small scale, not one of yards but of inches. In the sick bay Shukhov observes Kolya Vdovushkin, the young medical orderly, "writing lines of exactly the same length, leaving a margin and starting each one with a capital letter exactly below the beginning of the last. He knew right off, of course, that this wasn't work but something on the side" (20; *18*). What Kolya is doing, of course, is writing poetry. The informed reader sees him through the eyes of the uninformed Ivan Denisovich, and we have an instance of that Tolstoyan trope, "making it strange."

The temporal parameters of the narrative are set by the story's title. Although occasionally the hour of day (or night) is given, by and large the passage of time in the narrative is marked by reference to the routine of camp life: reveille, slop-out, breakfast, work parade, the march to the building site, dinner break, the march back, evening count, supper, evening roll-call, lights out. Ivan Denisovich possesses an instinct, a "clock in his guts," set to these immutable prison rhythms (164; *109*).

Shukhov must rely on his intestinal chronometer (or the sun) to tell the time because the privilege of measuring it belongs to the authorities: "Prisoners are not allowed clocks. The big boys tell the time for them" (21–22; *19*). It is the thermometer, not the clock, that the convicts keep their eyes on: when the temperature falls below −40 degrees, they are exempted from general duties.

Ivan Denisovich's ravaged body is a kind of calendar. He notes the passage of days by the growth of his facial hair: "With his free hand he felt his face – his beard had come on fast in the last ten days. . . . It would be bath day again in three days time" (22; *19*). (Thus we learn that prisoners are allowed to wash twice a month – an example of narrative economy typical of Solzhenitsyn.) The years of hard living have left their mark on his face and hands: his jaw was shattered on the river Lopat when he was fighting the Germans (22; *19*); he lost some of his teeth from scurvy in 1943 at the Ust-Izhma camp (14; *14*); the skin on his fingers is so rough he can hold a glowing cigarette tip without burning himself (32; *25*); the skin on his face is "case-hardened" (38; *29*).

In the Special Camp, time is a precious commodity. It is not money but time that is the currency of camp life. Shukhov uses the ninety minutes between reveille and work parade to do chores for others – "to earn a bit on the side" (3; *7*). In the evening he joins the queue in the parcel hut to save Tsezar's time; for this service Tsezar

rewards him with bread. Time-wasting by another inmate is theft. A
tardy prisoner holds up the column of zeks returning to the camp: "It
was no joke – he'd robbed five hundred men of more than half an
hour of their time" (123; *83*). If we multiply 30 minutes by 500, we
arrive at the figure of 250 hours: the hapless Moldavian is guilty of
stealing a total of ten days from his fellow prisoners!

The cosmography of the camp also includes descriptions of smell,
color, and animal and plant life. Smell in this world is related to air
temperature. Cold air is a poor conductor of odor. Only when at the
end of the day Shukhov is back inside the relative warmth of the
barrack does he have one or two olfactory experiences: "a quick
glance and a sniff" tell him what victuals are contained in Tsezar's
food packet (160; *106*); the dishwater-like liquid in the tea bucket
reeks of "moldy wood pulp" (163; *108*). We note that no reference is
ever made to the stench of the latrine bucket in the barrack: the
human nose is quick to get used to the most unpleasant odors when
it has been exposed to them for any length of time.

Nine colors are referred to in the text: black, yellow, white, blue,
green, red, brown, pink, and gray. The camp's basic color scheme is
composed of the blackness of the night, the whiteness of the snow,
and the brightness of the numerous yellow lights dotting the compound. Few of the other colors are vivid. The hues of dawn are
"blurry"; the gruel Shukhov eats at breakfast is "yellowish"; the glass
on the desk in the sick bay is "greenish"; the Tartar's blue shoulder
tabs are "grubby"; the Power Station is a "gray skeleton"; the sun is
"dim."

The fauna of this desolate place is comprised of the guard dogs,
the bedbugs that infest Shukhov's barrack, and the hospital cat. As
for vegetation, we learn that "wheat sprouts only in the bread-
cutting room, oats put out ears only in the food store" (75; *52*). "Not
so much as a sapling to be seen out on the steppe" (40; *31*). Fence
posts, not trees, stand tall in the white expanse of snow.

In this barren, flat, cold, colorless hell, Shukhov has learned to
survive. "Survival . . . is an act of refusal and resistance, and the

survivor's capacity to bear inhuman hardship, his small victories against the monolith of destruction, are the forms of life-inspired stubbornness," writes Terence des Pres.[15] This scholar has much to say about the moral and human value of dignified endurance under extreme conditions as exemplified by Ivan Denisovich and Solzhenitsyn's other heroes. We might add that the survival techniques Shukhov has developed, both by emulating others and by using his own wits and skills, are in themselves manifestations of his indomitable spirit, testimony to his abiding humanity. There is a strange poetry in the descriptions of the ways in which Prisoner Shch-854 uses his meager rations and his threadbare clothes to defeat the elements. In one of the story's most touching scenes, Ivan Denisovich experiences a kind of rapture while drinking and ingesting a bowl of skilly (152–53; *101*). In Book 9 of the *Republic* Plato describes the processes whereby man is restored to a natural condition: eating when hungry, sleeping when tired, regaining one's health when ill. Such sensuous pleasures, he declares, "are mere shadows and pictures of the true," which is "wisdom and virtue."[16] Unbeknownst to himself, Shukhov has disproved the ancient philosopher, for he has learned to invest the simple act of eating (or recovering from a chill) with "wisdom and virtue."

Ivan Denisovich is not given to moral introspection or theological speculation. He does not have a personal theodicy – an explanation for the way the unlimited goodness of an all-powerful God may be reconciled with the reality and prevalence of evil. He never asks the question Hannah Arendt posed: "Where was God in Auschwitz?" He is skeptical of the efficacy of prayer: "Prayers are like petitions – either they don't get through at all, or else it's 'complaint rejected,'" he tells the Baptist Alyoshka (175; *116*). We all know that Hell is a place of eternal punishment, where the sinner's soul shall know no surcease from its torments. It would appear that for Shukhov at least the Special Camp is just such a place, whence prayers do not reach God.

In fact, Shukhov's worldview is irrational and mythological rather than that of an informed religious believer. He asks Buynovsky, Gang 104's resident atheist, "How can anybody not believe in God when it thunders?" (116; 79). His fellow peasants, he informs his scientifically minded interlocutor, think that God breaks up the moon to make stars. In the debate about the extent to which the Russian people are truly religious, begun by the mystically inclined Nikolai Gogol and the radical critic Vissarion Belinsky in 1847,[17] Solzhenitsyn appears to side with the latter!

Andrei Tyurin, the tough foreman, believes in the Old Testament God of vengeance, Who punishes men for the evil they do. The officers who discharged him from the army for being a kulak's son were shot during the Great Terror. When he learned this, Tyurin recalls, "I crossed myself and said, 'So you're up there in heaven after all, Lord. You are slow to anger, but you hit hard.'"[18] Yet as he also remarks, "Proletarians or kulaks, it made no difference in '37. Or whether or not they had a conscience" (89; 61–62). The "meek and mild" Alyoshka's faith is very different from Tyurin's muscular variety: "We must pray for spiritual things, asking God to remove the scum of evil from our hearts" (176; 116).

For Shukhov, however, the idea of God as judge or redeemer is foreign: "I'm not against God, see. I'm quite ready to believe in God. But I just don't believe in heaven or hell. Why do you think everybody deserves either heaven or hell?" (177; 117). Ivan Denisovich may live in a place designed by evil minds to operate according to the "law of the taiga," but he refuses to accept that any human being deserves eternal damnation – or eternal bliss. His quiet, questioning words are an expression of his instinctive defiance – not of God, but of the System that has declared him and his fellow prisoners to be political sinners and consigned them to this icy inferno.

"The earth that wakes *one* human heart to feeling / Can centre both the worlds of Heaven and Hell" (Emily Brontë). Ivan Denisovich's heart is never dead to feeling. In a man-made hell he has retained his moral autonomy and human dignity: he is, in fact, a free man.

NOTES

1. Every morning, before the column of prisoners sets off to the work sites, the escort commander recites "the convict's daily 'prayer'": "One step to the right or left will be considered an attempt to escape and the guards will open fire without warning!" (39; *30*). This and all other quotations from *One Day in the Life of Ivan Denisovich* are taken from H. T. Willetts's English translation (New York: Noonday/Farrar Straus Giroux, 1991). The page reference to the Willetts translation is given first, followed, in italics, by a reference to the corresponding Russian text in Aleksandr Solzhenitsyn, *Sobranie sochinenii*, vol. 3 (Vermont and Paris: YMCA Press, 1978).

2. Aleksandr I. Solzhenitsyn, *The Oak and the Calf: Sketches of Literary Life in the Soviet Union* (New York: Harper and Row, 1980), p. 457.

3. The relationship between the artist and a tyrannical state is debated by Tsezar and Prisoner Kh-123 (84; *59*).

4. Aleksandr I. Solzhenitsyn, *The Gulag Archipelago 1918–1956: An Experiment in Literary Investigation*, 3 vols. (New York: Harper and Row, 1973–78), 1:x.

5. Il'ia Zil'berberg, *Neobkhodimyi razgovor s Solzhenitsynym* (Sussex: Author's edition, 1976), pp. 51–52.

6. Alice K. Turner, *A History of Hell* (New York: Harcourt Brace, 1993), p. 98.

7. *The Complete Prose and Poetry of John Milton* (New York: Modern Library, 1950), p. 131.

8. Ibid.

9. Solzhenitsyn, *The Gulag Archipelago* (1978), 3:59. *One Day* may be read as a companion book to part 5, chapter 3 (volume 3) of *The Gulag Archipelago*.

10. John Keegan, *A History of Warfare* (New York: Knopf, 1993), p. 164.

11. "Matryona's Home," *The Portable Twentieth-Century Russian Reader*, ed. Clarence Brown (Harmondsworth: Penguin, 1985), pp. 450–51.

12. Solzhenitsyn, *The Oak and the Calf*, p. 45. A Soviet journalist who in the winter of 1962 visited Solzhenitsyn in Ryazan wrote: "He was dressed in a padded jerkin and a fur hat with its ear-flaps and straps hanging down undone. I was astonished to be reminded of Ivan Denisovich" (quoted in Michael Scammell, *Solzhenitsyn* [New York: Norton, 1984], p. 457).

13. The signal for work parade, which reaches Shukhov's ears when he is

in the sick bay, "could barely be heard through double windows shuttered by white ice" (23; 20).

14. *Measure for Measure* 3.1.115–23.

15. Terence des Pres, "The Heroism of Survival," *Aleksandr Solzhenitsyn: Critical Essays and Documentary Materials*, ed. by John B. Dunlop, Richard Haugh, Alexis Klimoff, 2nd ed. (New York: Collier, 1975), p. 46.

16. *The Republic of Plato*, 2 vols. (Oxford: Clarendon, 1908), 2:585 D.

17. In his book *Selected Passages from Correspondence with Friends* (1847) Gogol idealized the Russian peasant as a humble and pious rustic; Belinsky declared in response that "by nature the Russians are a profoundly atheistic people. There is still a good deal of superstition in them, but not a trace of religious spirit" (see Vissarion Belinsky, "Letter to Gogol," in *Russian Philosophy*, ed. James M. Edie et al., 3 vols. [Knoxville: University of Tennessee Press, 1987], 1:316).

18. This was one of the passages Solzhenitsyn was asked to delete after he had submitted *One Day* for publication in the journal *Novy Mir*. The writer refused to comply: "What they were suggesting was that I should make concessions at the expense of God and of the peasant, and this I had vowed never to do" (Solzhenitsyn, *The Oak and the Calf*, pp. 43–44).

Who Is Ivan Denisovich?
Ethical Challenge and Narrative
Ambiguity in Solzhenitsyn's Text

DARIUSZ TOLCZYK

The revolutionary significance of Solzhenitsyn's *One Day in the Life of Ivan Denisovich* in the context of official Soviet culture did not arise from the novelty of the concentration-camp topic presented in Solzhenitsyn's work. This theme had in fact been present in Soviet literature when these penal institutions were being established in the 1920s and 1930s. Moreover, it reached high prominence in official Soviet literary discourse with the publication of Gorky's reportage from the Solovki concentration camp in 1929,[1] followed by the triumphant collective volume on the White Sea Canal project in 1934, authored by Gorky and thirty-five other Soviet writers, including such prominent literary figures as Viktor Shklovsky, Mikhail Zoshchenko, and Alexei Tolstoy.[2] The camps were presented in these works as benevolent institutions in which the Soviet government reeducated and resocialized individuals who had not adjusted sufficiently to life in Stalin's brave new world of five-year plans and the forced collectivization of property as well as minds. This peculiar form of resocialization through hard labor, hunger, and deprivation was known in the Soviet Union of the early 1930s by the euphemistic name of *perekovka* ("reforging"). Needless to say, there are no victims in these Soviet literary descriptions of Stalinist prison camps. The convention that presented incarceration in the camps as a successful form of Soviet "social medicine" naturally had no room for any mention of the physical or moral destruction of the "patients." In the literary reportages from Solovki and

White Sea Canal, prisoners not only do not complain about their fate but even express appreciation for the regime's initiative in putting them to work in the camps. Since the "reforged" camp prisoners were expected, in these literary accounts from the late 1920s and early 1930s, to evolve toward virtual self-identification with the Soviet regime, the success of the *perekovka* was predicated on the belief in a foreseeable future when there would be no more individuals in need of "reforging" and the system of reeducation would become obsolete. But the massive escalation of Soviet terror against ever-increasing numbers of alleged "enemies of the people" in the late 1930s contradicted these assumptions, and the whole *perekovka* concept was abandoned by the Soviet regime, making the very subject of the concentration camps taboo for more than two decades.

This lasted until November 1962 when, for the first time in Soviet literary history, the Soviet prison-camp experience was addressed in a literary work from the victim's point of view. Once again, however, it was not *One Day in the Life of Ivan Denisovich* that broke the silence and introduced this new perspective. Just a few days before publication of *One Day*, the newspaper *Izvestiia* printed a short story entitled "Samorodok" (A nugget)[3] from a semi-autobiographical cycle *Kolymskie zapisi* (Kolyma notes) by a now-forgotten writer and survivor of the Kolyma camps, Georgii Shelest.[4] Within a short time other soon-to-be-obscure authors, such as Iurii Piliar, Boris D'iakov, and Andrei Aldan-Semenov, followed suit with accounts on the same theme.[5] Thus Solzhenitsyn was by no means alone in giving expression to the prison-camp theme in officially published Soviet literature during the "thaw" of the early 1960s.

Yet what set Solzhenitsyn apart from the other Soviet writers who addressed the prison-camp topic at this time was that he alone succeeded in liberating this theme from specifically Soviet literary conventions and, more generally, in breaking free from a type of public discourse that had deprived the experiences depicted of materiality and reduced them to mere illustrations of abstract ideological constructs. True, all the officially published Soviet literary portrayals of the prison-camp experiences that appeared in the early 1960s dispensed with Gorky's ideological rationalizations as well as with the euphemistic manner of presentation he had used, showing the horrors of practical communism in ways that were sometimes even more shocking than the scenes portrayed in *One Day*. But at the same time, none of them managed to refrain from offering specific and clear-cut resolutions of all moral issues raised by the topic at hand. The constant readiness on the part of Shelest, Piliar, D'iakov, and Aldan-Semenov to dismiss the moral challenges presented by the camps per se by means of facile ideological statements produced a situation where the camp experience did not seem to have enough significance to unsettle the protagonists seriously, to say nothing of transforming them. These writers thus failed to uncover the sources of human behavior that could be revealed in this traumatic test of the limits of humanity. What is especially characteristic of these officially approved works is that the victim's point of view, introduced here, was in fact limited to only one type of victim, an ardent Communist for whom the main moral question raised by his imprisonment was not "Why do human beings do this to other people?" but "Why is this being done to me, a good and loyal Communist?" The conclusion of D'iakov's semiautobiographical *Povest' o perezhitom* (The tale of what I lived through) is symptomatic of these works. D'iakov's protagonist is speaking:

> Do you remember how restlessly we tried to understand what was the root of this evil, and who was to be judged by whom? Now we understand. Stalin, intoxicated by his power, treated his own people as enemies, and punished them. But finally the Twentieth Party Congress came, and it transformed our lives. I feel as if all these innocent victims were finally brought home by Lenin.[6]

This and other works of the officially sanctioned Soviet prison-camp prose of the early 1960s demonstrated that the ideological jargon of Soviet public discourse had created cognitive, axiological, and communicative filters unpenetrable for some writers even in the face of an experience of such devastating magnitude as the concentration camp.

In contrast, Solzhenitsyn's *One Day* brought to Soviet literary and public discourse a work that was to test the nature and limitations of this discourse in ways unprecedented and unrepeated until the advent of *glasnost*. Specifically, the human experience of the prison camp is presented here as an open ethical issue to be confronted by readers directly and individually. After four decades of Soviet totalitarianism, its chief experience – the horror of concentration camps – was here shown as a moral question in and of itself, not as part of an official answer to some other abstract and allegedly more important question concerning the speed of achieving socialism, the comparisons between Stalin's and Lenin's political agendas, and so on. In Solzhenitsyn's work, for the first time in Soviet history, Soviet readers were invited to face the most dismal aspect of their own reality without the ideological guidance that, in all other Soviet works concerned with the camp topic, had always been there to reconcile them with this reality. In *One Day*, Soviet readers were required to act as ethical judges, to reflect morally on a phenomenon crucial not only in terms of the Soviet social experiment but, in the more general sense, in terms of the twentieth-century experience of "humanity in extremis": on the ultimate test of human values confronted by dehumanizing forces of overwhelming magnitude.

Such an ethical challenge is inherent in the very subject matter of prison-camp literature, whether it is spelled out in explicit moral terms or not. The presence of an innocent victim, once it is acknowledged, automatically introduces an element of ethical anxiety to any situation where this plays a role. In this sense, the concentration camp is but a particularly vivid example of such an ethically charged situation. When official Soviet literature dealt with issues of victimization in general and the prison-camp experience in particular, it always provided an authoritative resolution, and thus either obliterated or neutralized the ethical challenge posed by the subject matter. In this paradigm, the presence of the victim is typically explained as part of some larger and more abstract context within which the very definition of victimhood is questioned and reevaluated. The accounts of the prison camps produced by Shelest, D'iakov, Piliar, and Aldan-Semenov managed to reserve the right to victimhood and innocence exclusively for those inmates who shared the value system of their Soviet oppressors and thus were always ready to accept their own victimization as an unfortunate but ultimately justifiable part of the larger, essentially positive context of the Soviet road to communism.

In this context, Solzhenitsyn's *One Day in the Life of Ivan Denisovich* is the only work that neither provides nor suggests clear authorial resolutions for the ethical problem inherent in the prison-camp experience. This absence is a result of a literary strategy assumed by the author and fulfilled with uncompromising discipline. Solzhenitsyn's short novel is unique in that it does not contain in its structure a communicative entity, a point of view or a voice, capable of presenting an ultimate authorial assessment of the ethical issues raised in the text. Though *One Day* is technically a third-person narrative, the perspective is in fact closely attached to the point of view of the novel's main protagonist, Ivan Denisovich Shukhov, a simple peasant-soldier serving his sentence for uncommitted crimes. His presence within the text is constant, and virtually the entire testimony of the camp experience is filtered through his consciousness. Thus the only commentary that *One Day* provides on the prison-camp experience is generated by Ivan Shukhov, a character hardly capable of and generally not interested in developing abstract arguments in order to define his fate. Moreover, this limited point of view is rendered by means of the narrative technique of *erlebte Rede*[7]: the verbal account of the camp is not only sifted through the cognitive filter of the central character, but its very formulation is colored and influenced by his linguistic competence. The language of the Russian peasant, that is, the language spoken by the "human material" of Soviet history and not by its designers, provides the descriptive medium by means of which Solzhenitsyn portrays the reality of the Soviet totalitarian experience. Thus a reader who would approach this work with thecustomary Soviet expectation of being guided by some ideological argument to a resolution of the potential anxieties generated by the text is bound for severe frustration. Ivan Denisovich does not speak the language of ideological generalization, and the author himself remains silent and distant behind his protagonist.

Solzhenitsyn's literary strategy demands the reader's active role in providing some sort of philosophical response to the ethical problems raised in the text. Yet no final resolution is possible, only a specific dialogue between a particular reader and the text, while the text itself remains open to other dialogues. Solzhenitsyn was absolutely unique in Soviet literature in establishing such a dialogical, open-ended communicative link between the reader and a text on a topic so explosively subversive for the Soviet authorities.

One Day in the Life of Ivan Denisovich thus clashed frontally with a Soviet public discourse that was incapable of tolerating open-ended issues, seeing them only as potential sources of dissent and controversy. Since each social and human phenomenon had to be fully explicable in the ideological terms of a regime claiming omniscience and moral superiority, Solzhenitsyn's work had to be supplied with interpretations and explanations formulated in the language of accepted Soviet public discourse. For this reason, *One Day* became a catalyst for numerous statements made in the Soviet press in which all the philosophical and rhetorical means available were mobilized in an attempt to neutralize the ethical challenge posed by Solzhenitsyn's work. These attempts failed, thus proving, for the first and only time in the history of Soviet public discourse, that the ideological resources necessary for the ethical and cognitive rationalization of the Bolshevik evil had been already exhausted by the Soviet regime and that, at the same time, this regime remained incapable of a searching look at its own ethical legitimacy.

In an interview granted in March 1967 to a Slovak journalist, Pavel Licko, Solzhenitsyn defined his own views on the principal tasks of a writer:

> By intuition and by singular vision of the world, a writer is able to discover far earlier than other people various aspects of social life and can often see them from an unexpected angle. This is the essence of talent. Talent, however, imposes certain duties. It is incumbent upon a writer to inform society of all that he is able to perceive and especially all that is unhealthy and a cause for anxiety. I was brought up with Russian literature and only circumstances prevented me from pursuing more extensive studies. . . . Russian literature has always been sensitive to human suffering.[8]

And in another segment of the same interview, Solzhenitsyn added:

> I know that the easiest thing for a writer is to write about himself. But I have always felt that to write about the fate of Russia was the most fascinating and important task to be performed. Of all the drama that Russia lived through, the fate of Ivan Denisovich was the greatest tragedy.[9]

These two statements shed light on the author's intention as well as his awareness of his own craft. By stressing the social duty of literature (defined here in terms of the anxiety caused by human suffering) and by viewing Ivan Denisovich (a sufferer) as a representative type embodying the drama of the Russian historical fate, Solzhenitsyn identifies himself and his work with the tradition of morally committed Russian nineteenth-century realism. The significant nature of the issues he raises within this literary tradition is reflected not only in the concrete historical circumstances he has chosen to describe but also in his general vision of human nature, and in this sense the actual circumstances of the concentration camp serve as the justification for larger philosophical questions. Just as the protagonist described in *One Day* is a particular example of the general moral drama engulfing all of Russia, so too can the drama of Russia be seen as a particular instance of an even more general trial – that of humanity degraded by the onslaught of totalitarianism. In this sense, *One Day in the Life of Ivan Denisovich* also belongs to the great twentieth-century literary tradition of prison-camp literature, a tradition that continually asks: How do human values stand up to the test of the totalitarian experience? What are the limits of human dignity and what are its sources?

As noted earlier, the focus of narration, the selection of the phenomena described in *One Day*, and the very language in which the image of the prison-camp experience is presented are essentially the products of the cognitive dynamics and linguistic competence of Shukhov himself. Ivan Denisovich is an insider in the dehumanizing world of the camps, and in this respect he is living testimony to the long-term results of man's confrontation with this special world. After years of being subjected to degradation and to a systematic assault on his self-image, his perception of the prison-camp experience contains an indirect answer to the question of the sources of human victory and/or defeat in the face of such extreme conditions. Hence the central ethical question of *One Day* is encapsulated in the problem of Ivan Denisovich's motivations: What is it that induces his actions and shapes his perceptions?

Seen in this context, the absence of drama in the tone and plot of *One Day* becomes a source of a meaningful ambiguity. The fact is that hunger, cold, pain, violence, injustice, and oppression – each more than sufficient as a source of shock and drama – permeate the reality of the prison camp Solzhenitsyn describes. It is only their status in the eyes of the central protagonist, who tends to perceive them as routine elements of everyday life, that deprives them of their dramatic potential. Shukhov, the "well-adjusted" insider, constantly understates the horror of his experience.

What, then, is the motivation behind this peculiar perception on the part of Ivan Denisovich? Is this matter-of-fact, tough-skinned view of the prison camp a necessary element in the struggle of a human being determined to survive and to save his dignity, a man who cannot afford to indulge in any dramatization of his fate since this could become psychologically disarming in the given conditions?[10] Or (to state the opposite possibility) is this perpetual under-statement and focus on the mundane practicalities of day-to-day existence in the camp, this systematic exclusion of the element of moral outrage, a reflection of an atrophied ethical sense in the pro-tagonist? Could it be an indirect indication of Ivan's inner submis-sion to slavery to the point of accepting his own victimization with-out a thought of protest? Is it an indication of Shukhov's confusion about what is wrong and what is normal? In other words, does *One Day* stand as a testament to the victory of human dignity over total-itarian dehumanization or to its ultimate defeat?

The question of Ivan Denisovich's ability to respond to the ethical challenge of concentration camp existence finds its most direct ex-pression in the dialogue between Shukhov and Alyoshka, a Baptist victim of Stalinist religious persecution. The topic of the conversa-tion is, precisely, the problem of identifying the sources of human values and relating the prison-camp experience to the value systems of the victims. Both prisoners express their understanding of how their experience of incarceration can be understood in light of the values they hold.

The importance of this dialogue as a key to the ethical dimension of *One Day* is indicated in at least two ways. It is the only major instance when Shukhov's habitual focus on the mundane and practi-cal aspects of his existence gives way to more "philosophical" reflec-tion. Moreover, the issue of Shukhov's own motivations in his life in the camp appears here explicitly as a theme. The significance of this episode is also suggested by the fact that it appears in the novel's conclusion. This privileged position gives the dialogue between Shukhov and Alyoshka the character of an interpretive key to the themes and events described in the whole work. The philosophical issues addressed here form a paradigmatic framework that allows the ethical dimensions of the phenomena described in *One Day* to be seen in proper perspective.

If Shukhov is a human puzzle owing to his limited verbal compe-tence and his inability to generalize from his own experience, his partner Alyoshka is just the opposite. Alyoshka views the individual as an ethical entity, that is, as someone who looks upon his own fate in the camp as the ultimate test of his value system. He expresses his value system in religious terms and defines his life as service to these ideals. Alyoshka's actions and words show his uncompromising observance of a fully internalized religious framework of values that encompass his entire identity. Even though he is physically confined to the prison camp with its dehumanizing pressures, Alyoshka is spiritually free because he psychologically inhabits a world beyond the power of the camp. This internal freedom, the source of Alyoshka's human dignity in the prison camp, is based on his rejection of that which is the main cause of all moral compromises in the camps – the illusive hope for survival and a change of fortune. That hope – which, according to such writers and prison camp veterans as Varlam Shalamov and Tadeusz Borowski, turns a prisoner into a slave[11] – in Alyoshka's case loses its tempting appeal.

Within the world of the prison camp, hope for survival often forces a prisoner to adhere blindly to the specific pragmatics of survival and either to internalize his oppressors' point of view, hoping for mercy or the "clarification of the mistake" (as in Shelest, Piliar, D'iakov, and Aldan-Semenov) or to acquire "camp smarts" and learn to live at the expense of his fellow prisoners (the typical attitude of criminals portrayed in nonofficial prison-camp literature).[12] The notion of hope is so foreign to Alyoshka that he not only seems to care little for the practical aspects of survival in camp but does not even allow himself to pray for a change of circumstances. When Shukhov tells him that praying in the camp is unlikely to shorten the time spent there, Alyoshka replies: "That's just the sort of thing you shouldn't pray for!" (177; *117*).[13] And it is this issue of hope that becomes the key subject of the climactic dialogue that sheds light on the human puzzle of the main protagonist, Ivan Denisovich Shukhov.

In contrast to Alyoshka, Shukhov has no clear-cut system of verbally defined values capable of serving him as a point of reference and a source of inner freedom in the camp. However, he indirectly acknowledges the need for something external to the realm of the camp experience. This point of reference appears as a traditional rhetorical entity, called "God," when Shukhov, lying on his bunk in the evening, sighs: "Thanks be to Thee, O God, another day over!" (174; *115*). Shukhov's purely rhetorical phrase here opens the conversation that will provide the main ethical paradigm of *One Day*: "Alyoshka heard Shukhov thank God out loud, and looked around. 'There you are, Ivan Denisovich, your soul is asking to be allowed to pray to God. Why not let it have its way, eh?'" (175; *115–16*). Shukhov answers: "Because, Alyoshka, prayers are like petitions – either they don't get through at all, or else it's 'complaint rejected'" (175; *116*).

The only desire Shukhov is intellectually capable of reflecting on is the hope for an improvement in his circumstances, with his release from the camp the peak of this desire. But he realizes the futility of this hope: "'Anyway,' he concluded, 'pray as much as you like, but they won't knock anything off your sentence. You'll serve your time from bell to bell whatever happens'" (177; *117*).

Alyoshka's answer opens a new dimension to Shukhov – that of a value-system that transcends hope.

> That's just the sort of thing you shouldn't pray for! What good is freedom to you? If you're free, your faith will soon be choked by thorns! Be glad you're in prison. Here you have time to think about your soul. Remember what the Apostle Paul says, "What are you doing, weeping and breaking my heart? For I am ready not only to be imprisoned but even to die in Jerusalem for the name of the Lord Jesus." (177–78; *117*)

In this central passage, Shukhov realizes that what he thought was the source of his everyday efforts and the direction of his life in the camp was not necessarily the hope for survival and freedom. In fact, just like Alyoshka, Ivan Denisovich himself has already abandoned this desire and has resigned himself to his fate in the camp:

> Shukhov stared at the ceiling and said nothing. He no longer knew whether he wanted to be free or not. To begin with, he'd

wanted it very much, and counted up every evening how many days he still had to serve. Then he'd got fed up with it. And still later it had gradually dawned on him that people like himself were not allowed to go home but were packed off into exile. And there was no knowing where the living was easier – here or there. (178; 117)

Unlike Alyoshka, however, Shukhov does not know what the source of his own behavior is in the camp, nor why he should abandon his hope and accept his fate. "'Look, Alyoshka,' Shukhov explained, 'it's worked out pretty well for you. Christ told you to go to jail, and you did it, for Christ. But what am I here for?'" (178; 118).

Both Shukhov and the reader (by virtue of Shukhov's limited scope of awareness) lack any explicit verbal definition of the particular values Shukhov himself may stand for in the camp. This absence of a clear philosophical assessment of the nature of Shukhov's true response to the camp experience establishes the principal ethical puzzle of One Day; namely, is Shukhov's acceptance of his fate a sign of his having transcended the enslaving dynamics of prison-camp life and, as in Alyoshka's case (but unconsciously), an indication of Shukhov's inner victory over totalitarian dehumanization? What, in that case, is the source of value that supersedes the hope for freedom and survival itself? Or is Shukhov's abandonment of any hope for freedom a reflection of the victory of the totalitarian machine? Is Ivan Denisovich recognizing the camp as his true home, the only framework of his identity, including his dreams? In such a case, Ivan Denisovich would exemplify a stance diametrically opposed to that of Alyoshka: he would represent a Soviet version of what Tadeusz Borowski has called the "Lagermensch,"[14] a type of camp prisoner whose body as well as spirit have become so accustomed to his circumstances that they refuse to travel beyond the barbed wire. And the appearance of the "Lagermensch" may well be totalitarianism's greatest victory over the human spirit.

Which of these two contradictory interpretations provides a more accurate answer to the question of what motivates Solzhenitsyn's protagonist? In other words, who is Ivan Denisovich? This is the question that each reader of *One Day in the Life of Ivan Denisovich* is invited to ponder long after the last page of the book has been turned.

NOTES

This article contains excerpts from Dariusz Tolczyk, *See No Evil: Literary Cover-Ups and Discoveries of the Soviet Camp Experience* (New Haven, Conn.: Yale University Press, forthcoming), used by permission.

1. Maksim Gor'kii, "Solovki," first published in *Nashi dostizheniia*, 1929, No. 6. Republished in Maksim Gor'kii, *Sobranie sochinenii*, 30 vols. (Moscow: Gosizdat, 1949–55), 17:201–32.

2. *Belomorsko-Baltiiskii Kanal imeni Stalina. Istoriia stroitel'stva*, ed. M. Gor'kii, L. L. Averbakh, and S. G. Firin (Moscow: Gosizdat, 1934). The following year the book was published in an English version: *Belomor: An Account of the Construction of the New Canal Between the White Sea and the Baltic Sea*, ed. Maxim Gorky, L. Auerbach, and S. G. Firin; Prepared from the Russian and edited, with a special introduction by Amabel Williams-Ellis (New York: Harrison Smith and Robert Haas, 1935; Reprint: Westport, Conn.: Hyperion, 1977). The English translation was presumably prepared in Moscow specifically for a Western audience, and for that reason it is much shorter than the original.

3. *Izvestiia*, November 6, 1962, p. 6. In *The Oak and the Calf: Sketches of Literary Life in the Soviet Union*, trans. H. T. Willetts (New York: Harper and Row, 1980), p. 44, Solzhenitsyn gives an account of this story's publication history. (The title here is rendered "Rough Diamond.")

4. Published in its entirety in *Znamia*, 1964, no. 9, pp. 162–80. The story published as "Samorodok" in *Izvestiia* appears here under the new title "Kolymskie samorodki."

5. See Iurii Piliar, *Liudi ostaiutsia liud'mi* (People remain people), in *Iunost'*, 1963, nos. 6–8 and 1964, nos. 3–5. Boris D'iakov's *Povest' o perezhitom* (The tale of what I lived through) appeared in *Oktiabr'*, 1964, no. 7. Andrei Aldan-Semenov's *Barel'ef na skale* (Bas-relief on a cliff) was published in *Moskva*, 1964, No. 7.

6. D'iakov, *Oktiabr'*, 1964, no. 7, p. 141.

7. *Erlebte Rede* is a German term that is variously rendered in English as "free indirect style," "indirect interior monologue," "quasi-direct discourse," and "narrated monologue." It refers to a conflation of third-person narrative with a strongly marked individual perspective identified with a particular protagonist. – Ed.

8. "One Day with Solzhenitsyn: An Interview by Pavel Licko" (first published in *Kulturny Zivot* [Bratislava], March 31, 1967), here cited from Leopold Labedz, ed., *Solzhenitsyn: A Documentary Record*, enlarged ed. (Bloomington: Indiana University Press, 1973), p. 38.

9. Labedz, *Solzhenitsyn*, p. 36

10. Solzhenitsyn directly commented on this subject during an editorial discussion of his text by the *Novy Mir* staff. "He who does not blunt his senses in camp will not survive," he is recorded as saying in Vladimir Lakshin's diary entry of July 23, 1962. "That's the only way I made it through. . . . If I had behaved like an intellectual, if I had been filled with inner turmoil, had fretted and taken to heart everything that took place, I would certainly have died." See Vladimir Lakshin, *"Novyi mir" vo vremena Khrushcheva: Dnevnik i poputnoe (1953–1964)* (Moscow: Knizhnaia palata, 1991), p. 67.

11. Tadeusz Borowski, a survivor of Auschwitz, writes:

It is . . . hope that makes people go without a murmur to the gas chambers, keeps them from risking a revolt, paralyses them into numb inactivity. It is hope that breaks down family ties, makes mothers renounce their children, or wives sell their bodies for bread, or husbands kill. It is hope that compels man to hold on to one more day of life, because that may be the day of liberation. Ah, and not even the hope for a different, better world, but simply for life, a life of peace and rest. Never before in the history of mankind has hope been stronger, but never also has it done so much harm as it has in this war, in this concentration camp. (*This Way for the Gas, Ladies and Gentlemen and Other Stories*, trans. Barbara Veder [New York: Viking, 1967], pp. 101–2)

Borowski's point is echoed by Varlam Shalamov: "Hope always shackles the convict. Hope is slavery. A man who hopes for something alters his conduct and is more frequently dishonest than a man who has ceased to hope" (See "Zhitie inzhenera Kipreeva," in Varlam Shalamov, *Voskreshenie listvennitsy: Rasskazy* [Moscow: Khudozhestvennaia literatura, 1989], p. 445. Here cited from "The Life of Engineer Kipreev," in Varlam Shalamov, *Graphite*, trans. by John Glad [New York: Norton, 1981], p. 135).

12. See, for instance, Gustaw Herling-Grudzinski, *A World Apart* (Oxford: Oxford University Press, 1951); Varlam Shalamov, "Na predstavku," in his *Voskreshenie listvennitsy: Rasskazy*, pp. 5–10 (translated as "On Tick," in Shalamov, *Kolyma Tales*, trans. John Glad [New York: Norton, 1980], pp. 107–12); and Borowski, *This Way for the Gas*.

13. The parenthetical page references are, respectively, to the H. T. Willetts translation of *One Day in the Life of Ivan Denisovich* (New York: Noonday/Farrar Straus Giroux, 1991) and to the Russian original as published in Aleksandr Solzhenitsyn, *Sobranie sochinenii*, vol. 3 (Vermont and Paris: YMCA Press, 1978). The page reference to the Russian text is given in italics.

14. See Borowski, *This Way for the Gas*, passim. The German word could be translated as "camp creature."

III  PRIMARY SOURCES

The Road to Publication

The Author's Perspective

One Day in the Life of Ivan Denisovich was written in 1959, a time when Solzhenitsyn, a former political prisoner and labor-camp inmate only recently cleared of all charges, was teaching high-school physics in the provincial city of Ryazan. Although he was an entirely unpublished author at this point, Solzhenitsyn had in fact been composing poetry, drama, and prose for more than a decade, all in deep secrecy and without the least hope of seeing any of these writings in print during his lifetime. In the excerpts that follow, Solzhenitsyn recalls the specific circumstances that led him to risk submitting the manuscript of One Day *– originally entitled* Shch-854 *after the main protagonist's prisoner identification number – to* Novy Mir, *the Soviet Union's premier literary monthly then edited by Aleksandr Tvardovsky.*[1]

Shortly before his death Tolstoy wrote that it is always immoral for a writer to publish in his own lifetime. We should, he thinks, write only for the future, and let our works be published "posthumously." Tolstoy reached his pious conclusions on this as on all else only after making the full round of sins and passions, but in any case, what he says is untrue even for slower epochs, and still more so for our swift-moving times. He is right that the thirst for repeated successes with the public spoils a writer's work. But it is even more damaging to be denied readers for years on end – demanding readers, hostile readers, delighted readers – to be denied all opportunity to influence the world about you, to influence the rising generation, with your pen. Quiescence means purity – but also irresponsibility. Tolstoy's judgment is ill-considered. . . .

For twelve years I quietly wrote and wrote. Only in the thirteenth did I falter. This was in spring 1960. I had written so many things, all quite unpublishable, all doomed to complete obscurity, that I felt clogged and supersaturated, and began to lose my buoyancy of mind and movement. I was beginning to suffer from lack of air in the literary underground. (*The Oak and the Calf*, pp. 12, 10)

I felt like one buried alive, and the friends from prison and prison-camp who occasionally dropped by were incapable of evaluating what I had written. My wife, while fervently admiring *The First Circle*, found *Ivan Denisovich* "boring and monotonous," while Lev Kopelev[2] judged it to be "typical socialist realism." At the time Kopelev was my only link to literary circles, but just as he had dismissed all the works I had brought back with me from exile in 1956, so now on a visit to Ryazan he rejected everything I had written since then, including *The First Circle*. Although I was certain that these judgments were wrong, after twelve years of solitary work I needed to hear someone else's opinion. I had lived in "free" Soviet conditions ever since my release from prison-camp, but I still felt like a captive in a foreign land. The only people I felt close to were fellow zeks, but they were invisible and inaudible, scattered all over the country. The rest of the population, in my eyes, consisted of the oppressive regime, the oppressed masses, and the Soviet intelligentsia – that *cultural milieu* which by its active mendacity participated in the system of oppression. I could not even imagine a milieu or social stratum where I would be read and appreciated. But of course there might be happy exceptions, isolated cases of meetings of the mind. My wife suggested that I try an experiment, allowing my works to be read by her friends, the Teushes – and in late summer of 1960 we made a trip to their cottage in the Moscow area.

[Veniamin Lvovich and Susanna Lazarevna Teush] indeed turned out to be a striking couple. Their conversation was fascinating. Veniamin Lvovich held unusual, incisive, and quite uninhibited opinions that went beyond politics to touch on spiritual matters,[3] while his wife possessed extraordinary charm, intellectual subtlety, and a kind of emotional iridescence. True, I also noticed that V. L. was somewhat slapdash in his ways. . . . But why should I care? It was only a question of whether I should give him a text to read. I decided to go ahead, handing the Teushes a manuscript entitled *Shch-854*, a politically barbed version of *Ivan Denisovich*, but the most harmless work I possessed at the time. For me this was an earthshaking step: I had never revealed myself to anyone whom I knew so little and of whom I was not yet deeply certain. My tightly sealed defensive shell had *by my own choice* developed a chink, the kind of opening through which the wind whistles as it carries away invaluable secrets. I had acquired two readers, yet I stood to lose the labor of my years in prison camp, in exile, and as a "free" man, along with my very head.

The reading had an explosive effect on V. L., who in his delight lost all peace of mind. He solemnly proclaimed the work not only a literary success but an historic event. And then he undertook a willful act: without even thinking to ask my permission, he called on his friend, assistant professor Kamenomostsky, and then on another academic . . . in order to read the text to them and to share his enthusiasm. Early on he also lent the work to his son. All these people joined him in expressing delight, while V. L. solemnly intoned Simeon's *Nunc Demitis*: "Lord, now lettest Thou Thy servant depart in peace." Teush and Kamenomostsky, unable to contain themselves any longer, thereupon came to see me in Ryazan. I was not told of [the others who knew of the manuscript] but simply confronted with the fact that Kamenomostsky had read the text. (Among the plaudits Teush and Kamenomostsky heaped on me was the declaration that they were touched by the gentle attitude of the main protagonist – and the writer – toward Tsezar Markovich.[4] And Kamenomostsky made a comment that struck me as very strange at the time: in his eyes, my work had through this trait "rehabilitated the Russian people.") And now they both expressed their eagerness to read anything else that I might have. What other works did I have in my possession?

I was thunderstruck by this unsanctioned disclosure. My heart sank, gripped by a feeling of a great misfortune, as though a fiasco had already occurred. What right did he [Teush] have?! But he stood there with an unaffected smile on his face as though nothing had happened: is not everyone delighted, after all? Ah, how painful it was to emerge from the underground! It took me several days to recover, but there was nothing to be done about it now. I had to get used to the idea of this breach, this sudden increase in the number of those who knew. There were no further unauthorized disclosures, and I gradually accustomed myself to the new circumstances.

In fact, no leak occurred, and I had now gained readers who were intelligent, sincere, and thorough. They immediately judged my text to be epic-making – for themselves, for Soviet literature, and for the country at large. How could an author – who, it must be confessed, had said similar things to himself – not be tickled pink? A small circle sprang up in which my works were read and discussed one after another. . . . And my decision to offer *Ivan Denisovich* to *Novy Mir* resulted not only from the momentum generated by the Twenty-second Party Congress,[5] but also from the dramatic success the story had enjoyed a year earlier in the narrow circle of Teusch and his friends. This "micro-success" gave me the certainty that *Ivan Denisovich* would be accepted by *non-zeks*. (*Invisible Allies*, pp. 34–36)

After the drab Twenty-first Congress, which damped and muted the splendid promise of the Twentieth,[6] there was no way of foreseeing the sudden fury, the reckless eloquence of the attack on Stalin which Khrushchev would decide upon for the Twenty-second! Nor, try as we might, could we, the uninitiated, ever explain it! But there it was – and not even a secret attack, as at the Twentieth Congress, but a public one! I could not remember when I had read anything as interesting as the speeches at the Twenty-second Congress. In my little room in a decaying wooden house where one unlucky match might send all my manuscripts, years and years of work, up in smoke, I read and reread those speeches, and the walls of my secret world swayed like curtains in the theater, wavered, expanded and carried me queasily with them: had it arrived, then, that long-awaited moment of terrible joy, the moment when my head must break water?

I must make no mistake! I must not thrust out my head too soon. But equally, I must not let this rare moment pass me by!

There was also a good speech at the Twenty-second Congress from Tvardovsky, and one theme he touched on was that although it had long since been possible to publish more freely and boldly, "we do not take advantage of the opportunity." *Novy Mir*, he hinted, might publish bolder and more polemical things, if only it had them. . . .

I decided to submit [*Shch-854*] to *Novy Mir*. (But for this, something worse would have happened. A whole year of claustrophobic nausea had worn me down to the point at which I must break out.)

I did not go to *Novy Mir* myself: my legs simply would not carry me, since I foresaw no success. I was already forty-three, and I had knocked about the world too much to call on an editor like a boy with his first story. My prison friend Lev Kopelev undertook to hand the manuscript in. Although there were six author's sheets[7] of it, it made quite a slim packet: typed, of course, on both sides, with no margins, and no spaces at all between lines.

I handed it over – and was gripped by the agitation, not of an ambitious young author, but of a hard-bitten camp veteran who has been incautious enough to leave a trail.

This was at the beginning of November 1961. . . .

There followed a whole month of misery in Ryazan: somewhere in the invisible distance my future was being decided, and I looked forward with growing certainty to the worst. Belief in change for the better is almost too much to ask of a veteran zek, one of Gulag's sons. Besides, after years of camp life you lose the habit of making your own decisions (in almost all important matters you drift helplessly with the tide of destiny), and get used to the idea that it is safer never to decide, never to take the initiative: you're alive – be satisfied with that.

Now I had broken the camp law, and I felt frightened. Besides, a new work was in progress, and all that I had done of it was in my apartment, which made the *Novy Mir* stunt seem even more obviously suicidal frivolity.

For all the fulminations at the Twenty-second Congress, for all the solemn promises to erect a monument to fallen zeks, or rather to the Communists among them – it has not been erected to this day – to believe that the time had come to tell the truth was simply impossible; our heads, our hearts, our tongues, have for too long been trained to avoid it. We meekly accept that we shall never speak the truth, nor shall we ever hear it.

However, a telegram arrived from Lev Kopelev at the beginning of December: "Aleksandr Trifonovich [Tvardovsky] delighted with article." ("Article" was our code word for the story: an article might be about anything – methods of teaching mathematics, for instance.) Like a bird flying smack into a pane of glass that telegram came. And my long years of immobility were over. A day later (on my birthday, as it happened), another telegram arrived, from Tvardovsky himself, summoning me to his office. And the day after that I went to Moscow, and superstitiously paused by Pushkin's statue as I crossed Strastnaya Square on my way to *Novy Mir* – partly to beg for his support, and partly to promise that I knew the path I must follow and would not stray from it. It was a sort of prayer. (*The Oak and the Calf*, pp. 13–14, 16, 18–19)

Solzhenitsyn learned that a key role in getting the manuscript into Tvardovsky's hands had been played by Anna Samoilovna Berzer, a member of the editorial staff of Novy Mir. *Without this maneuver, the work would almost certainly not have made its way into print.*

It was a year or so later that I was told how this had come about. The manuscript which I had preserved in deepest secrecy for so long had been left lying openly on Anna Berzer's desk for a whole week, without so much as a folder for cover, exposed to the first informer or sneak thief who came along. Anna Samoilovna had not been warned about the nature of the work. One day she began clearing her desk, read a few sentences, and saw that this was no way to keep such a manuscript, and indeed no place to read it. She took it home to read in the evening. She was shaken. She compared her reactions with those of her friend Kaleria Ozerova, an editor in the criticism section. They were identical. Knowing the ways of *Novy Mir* as she did, Anna Samoilovna reasoned that any member of the editorial board obedient to his conception of the magazine's best interests would block the manuscript, sit on it, swallow it – anything to keep it out of Tvardovsky's hands. So she had to use her ingenuity to toss it clear of all the heads between, lob it over the bog of caution and cowardice, and land it in Tvardovsky's hands first of all. Even then he might be put off by the manuscript's beggarly, dense and clotted appearance. Anna Samoilovna therefore asked to have it recopied at the magazine's expense. This took time. . . . But the most difficult part was outmaneuvering the other editors and breaking through to Tvardovsky, who usually did not want to see her and, quite unfairly, disliked her. (He somehow failed to appreciate her aesthetic judgment, her diligence, her selfless devotion to the magazine. All his authors were her friends, and forever hanging about the prose department.) Still, she knew very well the characters and weaknesses of all her superiors, and she began with the nearest of them, Yevgeny Gerasimov, head of the prose department. "There's a story about the camps. Will you read it?" The complacent Gerasimov, a voluminous prose writer himself, waved her away: "I don't want to hear any of that stuff about camps!" She tried the same question on the chief editor's second deputy, Aleksei Kondratovich, a little fellow so mauled and terrorized by censors that his ears seemed permanently pricked up and his nose permanently atwitch for the scent of danger. Kondratovich's reply was that he knew all there was to know about the camps, and didn't need any more telling. And anyway, he said, the thing couldn't be published. Next, Anna Berzer laid the manuscript before B. G. Zaks, the managing secretary of the editorial board, and shyly asked him to "take a look and see if you'd like to read it." She could not have phrased it more adroitly. For many years, Boris Zaks, a desiccated and tedious prig, had asked only one thing of literature – that it not interfere with the comforts of his declining years: his sunny Octobers in Koktebel and his enjoyment of the best Moscow concerts in winter. He read the first paragraph of my story, put it down without a word and walked away.

Anna Berzer now had every right to turn to Tvardovsky: the rest had all said no! She waited her chance – true, Kondratovich was present; she couldn't catch Tvardovsky alone – and told the chief that there were two unusual manuscripts which must be read by him personally: Lidia Chukovskaya's *Sofya Petrovna* and another one, about "a prison camp as seen through the eyes of a peasant, a work in which you could hear the voice of the Russian people." She had done it again; she could not have aimed more accurately at Tvardovsky's heart than she did in those few words. "I'll take a look at that one," he said immediately. . . . But Kondratovich woke up and jumped in. "Let me have it overnight. I'll read it first." He could not fall down on his job as protective filter for his chief.

He took it away, and realized from the first few lines that the mysterious nameless author (not putting my name to it seemed to me a way of slowing down any menacing turn of events) did not even know how to arrange the clauses of a sentence in proper order, and also used bizarre words. He had to take his pencil and scrawl all over the first page, the second . . . the fifth . . . the eighth, restoring subject, predicate and attributes to their rightful places. But the story proved to be illiterate from start to finish, and after several pages of this work Kondratovich gave up. What opinion he had formed by the following morning I do not know, but I think that it could equally well have been positive or negative. Tvardovsky, however, took the story away to read himself without asking what Kondratovich thought. Later, when I discovered what life at *Novy Mir* was like, I felt sure that *Ivan Denisovich* would never have seen the light if Anna Berzer had not shouldered her way through to Tvardovsky and hooked him with her remark that it was "seen through the eyes of a peasant." The chief's three guardian angels – Dementyev, Zaks and Kondratovich – would have gobbled up my Ivan Denisovich alive.

I cannot say that I had precisely planned it, but I did accurately foresee that the muzhik Ivan Denisovich was bound to arouse the sympathy of the superior muzhik Tvardovsky and the supreme muzhik Nikita Khrushchev.[8] And that was just what happened: it was not poetry and not politics that decided the fate of my story, but that unchanging peasant nature, so much ridiculed, trampled underfoot and vilified in our country since the Great Break,[9] and indeed earlier.

As Tvardovsky later told the story, he had gone to bed and picked up the manuscript. But after two or three pages he had decided that he couldn't read it lying down. He had got up and dressed. While his household slept, he had read through the night, with breaks for tea in the kitchen – read the story once, then reread it. . . . So the night passed, and what for peasants are the early morning hours arrived – but for literary persons it was still night, and Tvardovsky had to wait a little longer. He had no thought of going back to bed. After a while he telephoned Kondratovich and ordered him to ask Berzer . . . who and where the author was.

This led Tvardovsky to the next link in the chain, Kopelev, whom he now telephoned. He was particularly pleased to find that it was no hoax on the part of some well-known writer (though he had been quite confident about this) and that the author was neither a professional nor a Muscovite.

For Tvardovsky the days that followed were full of the joy of discovery. He rushed from friend to friend with the manuscript, calling for a bottle to celebrate the appearance of a new writer.[10] That is Tvardovsky for you: what makes him a true editor, an editor unlike others, is that he yearns to discover new authors, as feverishly, passionately, as any prospector longs to find gold. (*The Oak and the Calf*, pp. 19–22)

The View from *Novy Mir*

The diary entries of Vladimir Lakshin, literary critic and, from mid-1962, member of the editorial board of Novy Mir, *capture some of the tension and excitement that accompanied Tvardovsky's lengthy efforts to publish* One Day *in his journal.*[11]

Early December 1961

Spoke with Tvardovsky at the *Novy Mir* editorial office. He said he'd read an unusual manuscript – *One Day in the Life of a Zek*. He made me promise not to tell anyone about it and to return the manuscript in a day or two. "You'll see what this is all about and then we'll talk."

"All that is worthwhile in literature was achieved without permission from the higher-ups. As soon as you ask, 'May I?' they forbid it," reasoned Tvardovsky. It seems he is weighing the chances of publishing this text. . . .

Came home and that very evening began to read the story about the *zek*. Read it straight through without putting it down. My wife read it after me; I passed it to her page by page. Now *this* is authentic, powerful, and true! I think we got to bed only after three in the morning.

Who is this new author? . . .

Vladimir Lakshin became an official member of the Novy Mir *editorial board only in the summer of 1962, and was not involved in the journal's formal dealings with Solzhenitsyn until that time. In the spring of 1962, meanwhile, Tvardovsky had solicited comments on Solzhenitsyn's manuscript from several established writers, and had then forwarded the text, together with the responses he had gathered, to Khrushchev's aide Vladimir Lebedev. Lebedev had replied in a positive fashion but had made a number of requests and suggestions that needed to be discussed. To this end Tvardovsky called the editorial conference that Lakshin describes below.*

July 23, 1962

I arrived at the editorial offices, opened the door to Tvardovsky's office, and found a whole crowd around "my" large table set with bagels and tea. They were discussing Solzhenitsyn. Tvardovsky called me over, introduced me to the author, and invited me to take part in the conversation. . . .

Tvardovsky suggested – unobtrusively and with utmost delicacy – that he [Solzhenitsyn] take into account the remarks of Lebedev and Chernoutsan.[12] For instance, he might allot the Captain [Buynovsky] a bit more righteous indignation, take away the shade of sympathy for the Bendera followers,[13] or present one of the camp officials (a warder at least) in more conciliatory, restrained tones. They couldn't all have been scoundrels, after all.

[Aleksandr] Dementyev spoke more sharply and directly on the same subject.[14] He passionately defended Eisenstein and his *Battleship Potemkin*. He said that even from a purely literary point of view he didn't like the passages involving conversation with the Baptist. However, it isn't the literary aspects that bother him, it's the concerns pointed out earlier that give him pause. Dementyev also said (I objected to this), that it is important for the author to consider how his story would be received by former prisoners who had remained staunch communists even after the camps.

This touched a raw nerve in Solzhenitsyn. He responded that he hadn't thought about such a special category of readers and that he had no desire to do so. "There is a book, and there is me. Maybe I do think about readers, but only about readers in general, not various categories of them. . . . Besides, none of the people you refer to were on general duty. Depending on their qualifications or former position, they usually got jobs in the office or cutting bread, things like that. But the only way to understand Ivan Denisovich's situation is by working on general duty, that is, by knowing his situation from the inside. Even if I had been at the same camp, but had been an observer on the sidelines, I wouldn't have been able to write this. I couldn't have written it, and neither would I have understood what a saving grace work is . . . "

An argument ensued about the passage where the author speaks directly about the Captain's situation, saying that he – a sensitive, thinking individual – must turn into a dumb animal.[15] Solzhenitsyn wouldn't give in on this point either.

"But that's the most important point. He who doesn't blunt his senses in camp will not survive. That's the only way I made it through. I dread looking at a photograph of myself when I came out; I looked some fifteen years older than I do now, I was dull, sluggish, and my thinking was clumsy. But that's the only reason I made it. If I had behaved like an intellectual, if I had been filled with inner turmoil, had fretted and taken to heart everything that took place, I would certainly have died."

Over the course of the conversation, Tvardovsky unwisely mentioned the "red pencil" that might cut something out of the text at the last minute. Solzhenitsyn became alarmed and asked Tvardovsky to explain what he meant. Could the editors or the censor delete something without consulting with him? "The integrity of this piece is more important to me than having it published," he said.

Solzhenitsyn carefully noted down everyone's remarks and suggestions. He said that he divided them into three categories: those with which he could agree and which he even considered beneficial; those he would have to think over because they were difficult to decide; and, finally, those that were out of the question, since they involved changes with which he would not want to see the thing published at all.

Tvardovsky offered his own emendations meekly, almost bashfully, and whenever Solzhenitsyn spoke, he looked at him with loving eyes and agreed immediately if Solzhenitsyn's objections were reasonable. . . .

After some consideration, Solzhenitsyn agreed to make most of the changes requested by Lebedev, and shortly thereafter the revised text was sent to Khrushchev.[16]

October 8, 1962
Didn't write for a month, was on vacation in Bulgaria. A number of things have transpired during this period. Tvardovsky told me today that there had been some movement on the Solzhenitsyn front. While on vacation in Gagry, Khrushchev's aide V. S. Lebedev had picked a time and had begun reading the story to Khrushschev. He read to him again in the evening of the next day. The following morning all official business was put aside. Khrushchev summoned Mikoyan and the episode with the carpet dyers etc. was read aloud

once more.[17] Khrushshchev was greatly pleased and wanted to invite Tvardovsky down, but changed his mind for some reason.

There was a request for twenty-five copies to be printed immediately, presumably for discussion purposes. "Perhaps Khrushchev plans to give his colleagues an object-lesson on criticizing the cult of personality,"[18] speculates Tvardovsky.

"When that call came, my wife had dinner waiting, and she wanted me to hurry up. We tend to have a pretty austere style of doing things in the family, but at that point I called her from the kitchen, told her to drop everything she was doing, and gave way to emotion: 'Victory, Masha, victory!'

"I said to Lebedev, 'Thank you for being who you are and for helping us.' And he replied, 'Thank *you* for being who *you* are. You see, there is justice in the world, after all!' 'That may very well be so,' I replied, 'the point, however, is finding the right way to *present* it.'" The last words Tvardovsky pronounced in a very sly tone of voice. . . .

October 22, 1962
On October 20 Khrushchev received Tvardovsky. "I understood that the ice had begun to break up," recounted Tvardovsky. "They received me with the kind of good will I had never experienced before."

Speaking of *Ivan Denisovich*, Khrushchev declared that "it is a life-affirming work. In fact I'll go so far as to say that it expresses the Party spirit. If it had been written with less talent it would perhaps have been an erroneous thing, but in its present form it has got to be beneficial."

Khrushchev gave Tvardovsky to understand that not all members of the Presidium who had read the story had understood its essence. "But I told them, 'Go back and think it over some more.'"[19] . . .

Tvardovsky also spoke with Khrushchev about censorship. He told him that he considered it abnormal that after the Central Committee had entrusted him with the journal, an illiterate censor had been installed over him. "The censors would have just ripped *Ivan Denisovich* to shreds, isn't that so?"

"Yes indeed, they certainly would have," confirmed Khrushchev, with a cheerful laugh.[20]

November 3, 1962 [and later – A. K.]

. . . at about six o'clock we returned to the editorial office to celebrate the November 7 holiday with colleagues. . . .

The toasting and speech-making began. Tvardovsky made a few brief remarks, addressing everyone at the long, crowded table. He spoke of the joy of the November issue [of *Novy Mir*]. . . . Solzhenitsyn's name was on everyone's lips. We drank to his health and celebrated his story as a victory for the journal.

Tvardovsky had always said that he believed and held as his creed that every truly talented literary work would clear a path for itself. There is no work of genius written "for the drawer" which could not be published. *One Day* in this sense was the greatest test: not to have published it would have meant losing one's spirit of optimism, one's faith that in the final analysis everything would be put to rights. A writer must not blame the censor or his editor if his work is not published; he must blame only himself because he had not been able to make the work "victorious."

November 12, 1962

Over the holidays Tvardovsky reread Solzhenitsyn in page proof and later remarked at the editorial office, "I cannot believe that we are actually publishing this." He wrote a letter to the author with fatherly warnings and exhortations about the imminent sensation and the trials and tribulations of fame.

November 16, 1962.

Distribution of the journal has begun. . . .

A few days after the appearance of the November issue, a regular plenary session of the Central Committee [of the Communist Party] was held. The printers were asked to produce another 2,200 copies of the journal for sale at kiosks at the Plenum.

Someone cracked that the delegates wouldn't be discussing the official report because they would all be reading *Ivan Denisovich*. The journal was in fierce demand, it could be snatched right out of your hands, and people lined up to read it in the libraries from morning till night. Tvardovsky has been at the Plenum and says his heart had raced when he caught sight of the little blue books [of *Novy Mir*] throughout the hall.

The Censor's Notebook

Viktor Golovanov, an official of Glavlit, the Soviet censorship agency, had the specific responsibility of overseeing Novy Mir. *The meticulous record Golovanov kept of his activities gives a glimpse into the workings of the formidable machinery set up by the regime to control the printed word. His notes also highlight the highly irregular nature of the intervention on behalf of* One Day, *a work which the system would otherwise have doomed as a matter of course, almost certainly together with its author.*

Golovanov's journal came into Lakshin's hands some years after the censor's death, and Lakshin has published excerpts in his book "Novyi mir" vo vremena Khrushcheva *cited above.*

The following individuals are mentioned in Golovanov's journal entries: Pavel Romanov, the director of the Glavlit agency; Stepan Avetisian, his deputy; Galina Semyonova, head of the Fourth Department of Glavlit, the section overseeing fiction; Boris Zaks, Managing Secretary of Novy Mir; *Natalya Bianki, the journal's Production Manager.*

The text of One Day *was delivered to Golovanov "for preliminary reading" on October 23, 1962, and triggered the response indicated in the first entry cited below. Despite the dry bureaucratic style it is clear that Golovanov had instantly set off alarm bells which, in the context of the time, would normally have led to dire consequences for Solzhenitsyn. Golovanov obviously did not know that the book had already been cleared for publication at the highest levels of government. The bureaucratic system nevertheless required that he give his formal approval.*

After reading Solzhenitsyn's story on the evening of October 23, I reported to Comrade Avetisian on the morning of October 24 that this text had been received for review. Comrade Avetisian directed me to turn it over immediately to the head of the department. . . .

At 3:45 P.M. on October 30, the courier from *Novy Mir* presented two copies of signed page proofs for approval at the request of the secretary of the editorial board, Comrade Zaks. . . . The packet included A. Solzhenitsyn's story. . . .

The courier reported the following:

"When Comrade Zaks sent me over here, he said, 'If Comrade Golovanov will not authorize these materials for publication (he clearly meant the Solzhenitsyn story), have him return them to the editors without delay . . . '"

This peculiar ultimatum from Comrade Zaks was immediately reported by me to the head of the department, Comrade Semyonova, who instructed me to "grant approval without hindrance." I implemented this directive at 4:00 P.M., and the material was turned over to the courier.

The editorial manager Bianki said, "I know that this text was sent to the Central Committee of the CPSU, that Comrade Khrushchev has read it, and that an affirmative decision about publishing it was made by the presidium of the Central Committee."

Comrade Semyonova directed me to verify all this in the context of a formal meeting with Zaks himself, for which purpose he should be invited to the Glavlit premises. . . . I raised with Comrade Zaks the question of procedural aspects related to the publication of *One Day in the Life of Ivan Denisovich* by Solzhenitsyn.

Comrade Zaks stated the following:

"The text was received in unsolicited fashion some time ago. On Tvardovsky's initiative the editorial board then sent it to the Central Committee of the CPSU for comment. It was read by the First Secretary [N. S. Khrushchev]. Twenty-five offprints were then forwarded according to instructions. Next, and before the story was included in the November issue, Comrade Tvardovsky was received by the First Secretary, at which time Tvardovsky was informed that the possibility of publishing *One Day in the Life of Ivan Denisovich* was viewed positively." . . .

The head of the Fourth Section relayed the following instructions to me from Comrade Romanov, the director of Glavlit: "The text is to be authorized for publication without remarks or restrictions of any kind on the part of the censorship." The directive was carried out. I wrote a memorandum [on this matter] to Comrade Semyonova. . . .

At approximately 4:00 P.M. on November 16, at which time I was performing my duties as censor, the courier of the journal *Novy Mir* arrived at Glavlit USSR with the request that the November issue for 1962 be authorized for distribution. The request was granted immediately.

The Writer's Retrospect

Interviewed by the BBC's Russian Service in 1982 (the twentieth anniversary of One Day's *appearance in Moscow), Solzhenitsyn provided the following summary of the unique confluence of circumstances that had made the publication of this work possible.[21]*

For [*One Day*] to appear in print in the Soviet Union, one needed truly extraordinary circumstances as well as the participation of exceptional personalities. If Tvardovsky had not been the Editor-in-Chief of [*Novy Mir*], the work would certainly not have been published. And if Khrushchev had not been in power at this time, the publication could not have gone forward either. Nor would it have done so, moreover, if Khrushchev had not chosen this very moment to launch another attack on Stalin.

The appearance of my tale in the Soviet Union of 1962 could thus be compared to a phenomenon that defies physical laws, a situation where objects would rise instead of falling, or cold stones would grow hot of their own accord. It was impossible, simply impossible! The system was designed in such a way that for forty-five years it let nothing through, but there it was, confronted by this sudden breach. So it is clear that Tvardovsky, Khrushchev, and the specific circumstances had to interact in just the right way for the publication to take place.

Of course I could have sent my work abroad to be published there, but as I can now see from the reactions of Western socialists, if *One Day* had appeared [only] in the West, these people would have claimed that it was all a lie, that nothing of the kind had ever happened, that no prison camps had ever existed, and that no exterminations had occurred. That they remained silent is due solely to the fact that the text was published in Moscow with the approval of the Central Committee [of the Communist Party]; that's what shook them up.[22]

NOTES

1. The texts in this section are drawn from Aleksandr I. Solzhenitsyn, *The Oak and the Calf: Sketches of Literary Life in the Soviet Union*, trans. H. T. Willetts (New York: Harper and Row, 1980), and Solzhenitsyn's supplement to this work, *Invisible Allies*, trans. Alexis Klimoff and Michael Nicholson (Washington, D. C.: Counterpoint, 1995). World copyright © by Aleksandr I. Solzhenitsyn. English translations copyright © by HarperCollins Publishers, Inc., and Counterpoint Press, respectively. Reprinted by permission.

2. Lev Kopelev, a specialist in German literature, had been Solzhenitsyn's prisonmate in the late 1940s. (He served as the model for the character Lev Rubin in *The First Circle*.)

3. V. L. Teush, a retired mathematician, was a devotee of the anthroposophist Rudolf Steiner.

4. Tsezar Markovich, a well-supplied prisoner depicted in *One Day*, is an intellectual from Moscow who seems to be Jewish.

5. The Twenty-second Congress of the Communist Party of the Soviet Union, held in October 1961, represented the high-water mark in Nikita Khrushchev's campaign to discredit Stalin's legacy.

6. The Twentieth Congress was held in February 1956 and is remembered mainly for Nikita Khrushchev's sensational speech denouncing Stalin's crimes. The text of this speech was not published in the Soviet Union until the advent of Gorbachev's *glasnost* three decades later.

7. An "author's sheet," a unit of textual length used in the Soviet Union, contains forty thousand typographical characters.

8. Both Aleksandr Tvardovsky and Nikita Khrushchev were of peasant origin.

9. Reference to the forced collectivization of agriculture in the early 1930s.

10. For a vivid account of Tvardovsky's extraordinary behavior, see Vik-

tor Nekrasov, "Isaichu . . . ," *Kontinent*, no. 18 (1978): 3–5 (special supplement).

11. The selections are drawn from Vladimir Lakshin, *"Novyi mir" vo vremena Khrushcheva: Dnevnik i poputnoe* (Moscow: Knizhnaia palata, 1991). Copyright © by Vladimir Lakshin. Reprinted by permission of Svetlana N. Lakshina. Translated by Rebecca Park.

12. V. S. Lebedev and I. S. Chernoutsan, staff members of the Central Committee of the CPSU, had received Solzhenitsyn's manuscript from Tvardovsky and had read it before it was passed to Khrushchev (*Lakshin's note*).

13. The reference is to Ukrainian nationalist guerillas.

14. A. G. Dementyev, a literary critic and former Party bureaucrat, was a member of *Novy Mir*'s editorial board and functioned as a political adviser to Tvardovsky. For Solzhenitsyn's account of Dementyev's attack on *One Day*, see *The Oak and the Calf*, pp. 37–38.

15. The reference is to one of the few instances when the author's voice intrudes with an explicit comment that cannot be ascribed to Shukhov. Buynovsky is shown sitting motionless and devoid of thought after finishing his meal. He did not want to move: "Moments like this . . . were turning the loud and domineering naval officer into a slow-moving and circumspect zek: only this economy of effort would enable him to endure the twenty-five years of imprisonment doled out to him" (see *One Day in the Life of Ivan Denisovich*, trans. H. T. Willetts, p. 82; *Sobranie sochinenii* 3: 57).

16. Tvardovsky's highly respectful cover letter, dated August 6, 1962, together with Lebedev's September memorandum noting that Khrushchev had familiarized himself with Solzhenitsyn's text, were published in *Vecherniaia Moskva*, August 6, 1994, p. 4. (The same texts appear in *Kontinent*, no. 75 [1993], but are incorrectly dated. The August 6 date is confirmed by Lakshin, *"Novyi mir" vo vremena Khrushcheva*, p. 91.)

17. Lakshin's terse description is open to misunderstanding. Khrushchev is known to have admired the bricklaying scene in *One Day*, whereas the story of the carpet dyers could scarcely have appealed to him. In the second edition of Solzhenitsyn's *Bodalsia telenok s dubom* (Moscow: Soglasie, 1996), p. 66, Khrushchev is directly quoted as claiming he was moved by Shukhov's desire not to waste any mortar.

18. The phrase "cult of personality" was a Soviet euphemism used to characterize the excesses of Stalinism.

19. In his memoirs, Khrushchev reports that only Mikhail Suslov, the Party's chief ideologist, had been vocal in opposing the decision to publish *One Day*. See *Khrushchev Remembers: The Glasnost Tapes*, ed. and trans. Jerrold L. Schecter and Vyacheslav V. Luchkov (Boston: Little, Brown, 1990), p. 198.

20. This meeting signaled the final green light for the publication of *One Day*. It is noteworthy that it occurred on the very eve of the 1962 Cuban missile crisis. As Solzhenitsyn writes:

> Khrushchev did not, of course, know, as he chatted peacefully with Tvardovsky about literature, that blown-up photographs of Soviet rockets in Cuba were being mounted on display boards in Washington, to be shown to delegates at an OAS meeting on Monday, at which Kennedy would obtain consent to his unprecedentedly bold step: inspecting Soviet ships. Only Sunday stood between Khrushchev and his week of humiliation, fear and surrender. And it was on that very last Saturday that he issued *Ivan Denisovich*'s visa. (*The Oak and the Calf*, p. 42)

21. Aleksandr Solzhenitsyn, "Interv'iu dlia radio Bi-Bi-Si," *Vestnik Russkogo Khristianskogo Dvizheniia*, no. 138 (1983): 158.

22. The same point has been made by a number of commentators. See, for example, the remarks of the French scholar Georges Nivat in a round table discussion on Solzhenitsyn, "Chto znachit Solzhenitsyn dlia kazhdogo iz nas?," *Kontinent*, no. 18 (1978): 414–15.

Early Responses

After the publication of One Day in the Life of Ivan Deni-sovich *in November 1962, the Soviet press erupted in a veritable chorus of praise, but one that had clearly taken its cue from the blessing bestowed upon this work by the head of the Party.[1] Of greater interest, therefore, are the responses to manuscript copies of* One Day *collected by Tvardovsky several months earlier from a number of established writers and critics and used by him to support his appeal to Khrushchev.*

Two responses from this series are represented below. The first is by Kornei Chukovsky,[2] literary critic, translator, and celebrated writer of children's verse. The second is by Mikhail Livshitz,[3] a Marxist critic with populist sympathies who at one point had been a close associate of Tvardovskys, and who here strives to place One Day *and the tragedy it depicts within the theory of progress enunciated by Engels.*

Kornei Chukovsky, "A Literary Miracle"

Shukhov exemplifies the character traits of a simple Russian man: steadfastness in life, feisty stubbornness, the ability to be a jack-of-all-trades, stamina, and a cunning blended with kindness. In this sense he is close to Vasili Tyorkin.[4] Although Shukhov's story is narrated in the third person, the entire text is presented in *his* idiom, a language that is colorful, pithy, and full of humor. The author does not flaunt linguistic oddities in the manner of Dahl, Melnikov-Pechersky, or Aleksei Remizov, nor does he dish up juicy lexical tidbits in the tasteless manner of Leskov. His speech is not stylized – it is alive and organic, as free and natural as breathing itself, a marvelous popular speech with an admixture of prison-camp slang. In fact the theme of this work could only have been broached by someone in total control of this idiom. The theme is the baneful spirit of torture that had become institutionalized in human relationships:

the torments that were inflicted upon absolutely innocent people for years on end by organized and armed villains. Shukhov, just like his fellow inmates, had committed no crime, and he was forced into declaring himself a traitor by torture and vicious beatings. With a single exception, none of the other zeks are guilty of the slightest transgression either. They are "made-up spies, make-believe spies. Their papers had them down as spies, but they were just ex-prisoners of war." An author with less talent would surely have stressed this with journalistic abandon, cursing and rending his clothes. But A. Ryazansky's[5] greatest strength lies precisely in the way he has not given vent to a passionate rage. He is a chronicler, not a journalistic commentator. In a voice that is steady, unhurried, and calm, he methodically records the thoughts and actions of Shukhov who, by virtue of this tenacious and brilliantly stubborn personality, can even find contentment amid the lawlessness, violence, and contempt for human dignity to which he is constantly subjected. In effect the story could have been entitled "A *Happy* Day in the Life of Ivan Denisovich." But of course the author's tragic irony does not need further emphasis: it can be clearly felt on every page.

In a word, this story marks the appearance of a powerful, original, and mature talent in our literature. One scene alone – Ivan Shukhov at work and carried away by the process – I think deserves the adjective "classic." And at every point the author chooses the path of greatest resistance, and everywhere he achieves victory. It would of course be terrible if the editors decided to introduce "corrections" into this text. . . .[6] And I shudder to think that this wonderful tale might remain unpublished. It contains nothing that could offend the censors. It condemns a *past* that is happily no longer with us. And it is written entirely *in praise* of the Russian character. . . .[7]

Mikhail Livshitz, "On Solzhenitsyn's *One Day in the Life of Ivan Denisovich*"

I think that only a person whose conscience is overgrown with scar tissue could pass by this work with indifference. It is bigger than literature. Yet it is not a complaint: it is a calm and measured depiction of the tragedy of a people. Who is it that has written that the great tribulations which make up history occur only as a result of external oppression, war, famine, and epidemics? That would be much too simple. The story told by Tyurin, the foreman, and which I take as the climax of the entire narrative, explains why this is not so – and offers us a complete philosophy of history.

I like the fact that the author does not depict any extraordinary horrors. His work is not imitative in any sense, yet his Ivan Denisovich seems to have stepped out of the Russian literary classics in order to live in our day. One can trust this simple worker, and he can teach us a great many things – more important things than can be extracted from a Hemingway or a Camus. As bleak as everything described in *One Day* is, the story evokes courage, not doubt. I am reminded of the words Engels addressed to the Russian populist Danielson: "A nation as great as yours will survive any crisis. There can be no great historical misfortune that is not compensated in some way by historical progress. What varies is the specific manner in which this is realized."

It would take up a great deal of space to enumerate all the wonderful realistic details that seem to have been carved by the chisel of a master in this brief work. The story is a superb example of the way in which a large truth is embodied in a multitude of smaller truths which together add up to literary form. The author is also wise and profound in his psychological depictions, in his choice of words, and in his general view of life.

It would be a crime not to publish this story. It is a text that raises our level of consciousness. The Soviet regime will not be harmed by this process, but can only benefit from it.

Tvardovsky's preface to the publication of One Day *in his journal will serve as a sample of a more official type of early response.*[8] *His remarks represent an effort to harmonize his obvious admiration for Solzhenitsyn's work with a fervently expressed faith in the liberalizing potential of the Party.*

Aleksandr Tvardovsky, "In Lieu of a Foreword"

Aleksandr Solzhenitsyn's story is based on subject matter unusual for Soviet literature. It is a theme that brings back echoes of the unhealthy phenomena in our national development linked to the cult of personality – a phase now discredited and rejected by the Party and one that already seems to belong to a distant past, even though it is not far removed from us in chronological terms. Yet it is also true that the past, whatever shape it might have taken, can never become a matter of indifference for the present. Moreover, the only guarantee of a full and irrevocable break with those aspects of our past that cast a pall upon it is a truthful and courageous acknowledgment of the consequences to which it led. That is precisely what N. S. Khrushchev had in mind in his memorable concluding speech at the Twenty-second Party Congress: "It is our duty to look closely at the abuses of power in all their manifestations. In time we shall all die, for we are all mortal, but as long as we are active we can and we must find out the truth about a great many things, and inform the Party and the people. . . . And this we must do so that nothing of the kind can ever recur in the future."

One Day in the Life of Ivan Denisovich is not a memoir in the documentary sense. It does not represent reminiscences or notes detailing the author's personal experiences, even though only personal experience could have given this story its sense of authenticity and verisimilitude. It is a work of literary art, and precisely because it illuminates the given subject matter through art, it stands as testimony of particular significance. It is a document in art, one whose very existence – considering the specific material on which it is based – had until now seemed quite improbable.

In Solzhenitsyn's tale readers will not find an exhaustive description of the historical period that includes the bitter memory of 1937. The theme of *One Day* is limited in terms of time and place, as well as by the mental horizon of its main protagonist. But this single day in the life of the prison-camp inmate Ivan Denisovich Shukhov described for us by Aleksandr Solzhenitsyn (for whom this is the first publication) grows into an extraordinarily vivid picture, strikingly truthful in its depiction of human nature. Many of the individuals portrayed here in their tragic capacity as "zeks" can easily be imagined in different surroundings, be it on the front lines or in postwar construction projects. In fact they are the same kind of people one would meet there, except that the force of circumstances had thrust them into extreme conditions of harsh physical and moral travail.

This text does not focus specifically on the horrifying acts of cruelty and violence that took place as the result of the breakdown of Soviet legality. The author has chosen a most ordinary day in the life of the prison camp, tracing it from reveille to lights out. Yet the very ordinariness of this day cannot fail to evoke a bitter and painful reaction in reader's hearts as they contemplate the fate of the individuals who emerge with such vitality and warmth from the pages of this work. It is the writer's great achievement, however, that this bitterness and pain does not lead to a feeling of hopeless despondency. On the contrary, this work, so unusual in the unadorned and distressing nature of the reality it depicts, serves to unburden our souls by saying what had been left unsaid but needed to be said, strengthening and ennobling our spirit in the process.

This somber tale is more proof that in our time there are no aspects of life that are off limits to the Soviet writer or that cannot be truthfully depicted. It is all a matter of the resources the writer brings to the task.

One other simple and instructive conclusion can be drawn from this tale: When the subject matter is truly significant, when there is a faithfulness to the larger verities of life, and a deep humanity in depicting even the most painful subjects, this cannot fail but call to life the appropriate literary form. In *One Day* this form is strikingly unique by virtue of its workaday ordinariness and its unassuming appearance. It is entirely unselfconscious and therefore full of inner dignity and strength.

Although I have no wish to anticipate readers' reactions to this short work, I am convinced that it signals the arrival of a new, original, and fully mature talent on our literary scene.

It is possible that the author's use – moderate and appropriate though it is – of certain words and phrases characteristic of the milieu in which the protagonist spends his working day may evoke the objections of particularly fastidious readers. But on the whole *One Day* is the kind of work that elicits the heartfelt desire to share our feeling of gratitude to the author with other readers.[9]

* * *

The virtually unanimous acclaim with which the official Soviet press had greeted the appearance of *One Day* in November 1962 proved to be a short-lived phenomenon. Rapid changes were taking place in the ideological climate of the USSR in the aftermath of the Cuban missile crisis (October 1962), and by the spring of the following year a full-blown campaign to reestablish discipline and doctrinal orthodoxy in the arts was in progress.[10] It was therefore only a matter of months before *One Day* began to be criticized for its obvious lack of consonance with the Marxist verities, even though the literary critic Vladimir Lakshin still had the ability to publish a detailed polemical rebuttal of these attacks in the January 1964 issue of *Novy Mir*.[11] The increasing official disapproval was formalized in April 1964 when the Soviet committee charged with picking the winner of the Lenin Prize in Literature was heavily pressured to award the prize to a work other than *One Day*.[12]

But the responses of individual readers came to play a far more important role for Solzhenitsyn than the reviews in the official Soviet press. Apart from the high praise bestowed on *One Day* by such eminent readers as Anna Akhmatova and Varlam Shalamov,[13] Solzhenitsyn was particularly moved by what he called the "avalanche of letters" he received from former camp inmates. As he confided to Shalamov in the spring of 1963, he had by then already written some five hundred responses.[14] And this was by no means a question of courtesy alone: Solzhenitsyn was now engaged in gathering materials for *The Gulag Archipelago*, and many of the former zeks he contacted in this manner were to become the primary witnesses in his "literary investigation" of the Soviet prison and concentration camp system.[15] *One Day in the Life of Ivan Denisovich* thus made possible the writing of the work that George Kennan has called "the greatest and most powerful single indictment of a political regime ever to be leveled in modern times."[16]

If one looks outside the Soviet Union, perhaps the most direct evidence of the level of response to *One Day* is the staggering number of translations of this work that appeared worldwide within a few years of its publication in 1962. Apart from the several English translations discussed elsewhere in the present book, *One Day* was rendered into at least thirty other languages, including Albanian, Icelandic, and Malayan.[17] It seems that the only country in Europe that did not permit *One Day* to be published on its territory in the wake of the Soviet publication was East Germany, then ruled by the rigid doctrinaire Walter Ulbricht.[18]

NOTES

1. For a listing of the principal reviews, see Michael Nicholson, "Aleksandr Solzhenitsyn: A Bibliography of Responses in the Official Soviet Press from November 1962 to April 1973," in John B. Dunlop, Richard Haugh, and Alexis Klimoff, eds., *Aleksandr Solzhenitsyn: Critical Essays and Documentary Materials*, 2d ed. (New York: Collier Macmillan, 1975), pp. 581–610.

2. Chukovsky's evaluation appears in the commentary section of Lidiia Chukovskaia, *Zapiski ob Anne Akhmatovoi*, vol. 2 (Paris: YMCA Press, 1980), pp. 608–9. Copyright © by YMCA Press. Reprinted by permission. Translated by the editor. Chukovsky notes in his diary that Tvardovsky gave him the manuscript on April 9, and that he was so delighted by it that he wrote his review immediately (see Kornei Chukovskii, *Dnevnik 1930–1969* [Moscow: Sovremennyi pisatel', 1994], pp. 308, 310).

3. The Lifshitz review appears in *Voprosy literatury*, 1990, no. 7 (July), pp. 74–75. Copyright © by *Voprosy literatury*. Reprinted by permission. Translated by the editor.

4. Vasili Tyorkin is a cheerful and resourceful front-line soldier depicted in Tvardovsky's long narrative poem of the same name.

5. The manuscript was submitted to *Novy Mir* anonymously, and this pseudonym was devised at the *Novy Mir* offices by Lev Kopelev. (It reflected the fact that Solzhenitsyn was then living in Ryazan.) See Raisa Orlova, *Vospominaniia o neproshedshem vremeni* (Moscow: Slovo, 1993), p. 221.

6. Chukovsky here gives two examples of "substandard" grammatical usage that he considers entirely appropriate to the context.

7. Chukovsky ends his review with three sentences on purely linguistic aspects of the work.

8. Translated by the editor from "Vmesto predisloviia," *Novyi mir*, 1962, no. 11, pp. 8–9.

9. The hope for liberalization that in Tvardovsky's mind became linked with the fate of *One Day* is even more explicitly, not to say desperately, voiced in an interview published in *Pravda* on May 12, 1963. See the translation of this passage in Priscilla Johnson and Leopold Labedz, eds., *Khrushchev and the Arts: The Politics of Soviet Culture, 1962–1964* (Cambridge, Mass.: MIT Press, 1965), pp. 212–13. It is a measure of Tvardovsky's tormenting split between art and loyalty to the Party that in the following year we find him reading the works of Lenin in an attempt to find strength amid the mounting attacks on his journal. See Margareta O. Thompson, "Tvardovskii's Unpublished Letters to Makedonov," *Russian Language Journal* 48, nos. 159–61 (1994): 209.

10. See Johnson and Labedz, *Khrushchev and the Arts*, pp. 101–20, 137–86.

11. "Ivan Denisovich, ego druz'ia i nedrugi," *Novyi mir*, 1964, no. 1, 223–45. Partially translated as "Ivan Denisovich, His Friends and Foes," in Johnson and Labedz, *Khrushchev and the Arts*, pp. 275–88.

12. See Michael Scammell, *Solzhenitsyn: A Biography* (New York: Norton, 1984), pp. 493–95.

13. On Akhmatova's opinion of *One Day*, see Lidiia Chukovskaia, *Zapiski ob Anne Akhmatovoi*, vol. 2 (Paris: YMCA Press, 1980), e.g., p. 431; and Nataliia Il'ina, "Pechal'nye stranitsy," *Oktiabr'*, 1990, no. 10, 131–32. Shalamov's long letter on *One Day* appears in *Shalamovskii sbornik*, Vyp. 1 (Vologda, 1994), pp. 64–75.

14. *Shalamovskii sbornik*, p. 75.

15. Aleksandr Solzhenitsyn, *The Oak and the Calf: Sketches of Literary Life in the Soviet Union*, trans. H. T. Willetts (New York: Harper and Row, 1980), pp. 66, 90, 457. Solzhenitsyn has prepared a survey of both friendly and

hostile letters sent to him: "How People Read *One Day*," in Leopold Labedz, ed., *Solzhenitsyn: A Documentary Record*, enlarged ed. (Bloomington: Indiana University Press, 1973), pp. 44–67.

16. "George Kennan, "Between Heaven and Earth," in Dunlop, Haugh, and Klimoff, *Aleksandr Solzhenitsyn*, p. 505.

17. See Donald M. Fiene, *Alexander Solzhenitsyn: An International Bibliography of Writings by and about Him* (Ann Arbor, Mich.: Ardis, 1973), pp. 83–127.

18. See Willi Beitz, ed., *Vom 'Tauwetter' zur Perestroika* (Bern: Peter Lang, 1994), p. 137.

IV SELECT BIBLIOGRAPHY

Select Bibliography

Works by Solzhenitsyn most relevant to *One Day in the Life of Ivan Denisovich*

Solzhenitsyn, Aleksandr. "Odin den' Ivana Denisovicha. Povest'." *Novyi mir*, 1962, no. 11: 8–74.
  The first publication of *One Day*.
———. "Odin den' Ivana Denisovicha. Povest'." *Roman-gazeta*, 1963, no. 1: 1–47.
  The circulation of this biweekly publication surpassed 700,000.
———. *Odin den' Ivana Denisovicha*. Moscow: Sovetskii pisatel', 1963.
  In both this and the *Roman-gazeta* edition, Solzhenitsyn restored some of the cuts and other changes that were made for the *Novy Mir* publication.
———. *Odin den' Ivana Denisovicha. Matrenin dvor*. Paris: YMCA Press, 1973.
  In a prefatory note, Solzhenitsyn states that this is to be considered the definitive edition of *One Day* and "Matryona's Home." But he has nevertheless introduced several further (minor) changes into the text of *One Day* that are included in the Russian-language *Collected Works* (vol. 3, 1978).
———. *One Day in the Life of Ivan Denisovich*.
———. Translated by Ralph Parker. New York: Dutton, 1963.
  Parker's translation (in a somewhat different version) was first serialized in *Moscow News*, an English-language Soviet weekly.
———. Translated by Max Hayward and Ronald Hingley. New York: Praeger, 1963.
  This translation appeared simultaneously with the American edition of the Parker version.
———. Translated by Bela Von Block. New York: Fawcett, 1963.
———. Translated by Thomas P. Whitney. New York: Fawcett, 1963.
———. Translated by Gillon Aitken. Revised edition. New York: Farrar Straus Giroux, 1971.
  An earlier version appeared in 1970.
———. Translated by H. T. Willetts. New York: Noonday/Farrar Straus Giroux, 1991.

This is the only translation based on the canonical Russian text as published in Solzhenitsyn's *Collected Works*. The Willetts translation also appears in the Everyman's Library series published by Alfred A. Knopf in 1995. However, the introduction by John Bayley is filled with so many egregious errors that the Everyman edition cannot be recommended.

———. *The Oak and the Calf: Sketches of Literary Life in the Soviet Union.* Translated by H. T. Willetts. New York: Harper and Row, 1980.

Translation of *Bodalsia telenok s dubom: Ocherki literaturnoi zhizni.* Paris: YMCA Press, 1975.

This book gives the most detailed and authoritative account of the publication history of *One Day*, as well as focusing on Solzhenitsyn's complex relationship with Tvardovsky.

A second, considerably expanded edition of the Russian text was produced in 1996 by the Moscow publishing house "Soglasie." Additions include materials published in *Novy Mir* in 1991 concerning the individuals who had helped Solzhenitsyn in his literary tasks before his exile. The writer has called these previously anonymous helpers *"Nevidimki"* [the invisible ones]. In English translation these chapters have been published in book form as *Invisible Allies*, trans. Alexis Klimoff and Michael Nicholson (Washington, D. C.: Counterpoint, 1995). The additional material provides further detail on *One Day*.

———. *Sobranie sochinenii*, 20 vols. Paris and Vermont: YMCA Press, 1978–91.

This edition of Solzhenitsyn's *Collected Works* was overseen by the author. It does not include *The Oak and the Calf* and a number of essays and public statements that appeared after 1983.

The canonical version of *One Day* appears in volume 3 (1978).

———. *The Gulag Archipelago, 1918–1956: An Experiment in Literary Investigation.* 3 vols. Translated by Thomas P. Whitney (vols. 1–2) and H. T. Willetts (vol. 3). New York: Harper and Row, 1973–78.

Contains many references to *One Day*, often in the form of relating the experience of Ivan Denisovich as depicted in *One Day* to the circumstances being described in *Gulag*. At one point Ivan Denisovich takes over the narration to give his views of camp mores (see 2:214–16, 223–26).

General works on Solzhenitsyn

Brown, Edward J. "Solzhenitsyn and the Epic of the Camps." In his
Russian Literature since the Revolution, pp. 260–91. Cambridge,
Mass.: Harvard University Press, 1982.
  Perhaps the best brief overview of Solzhenitsyn's works available
  in English.

Canadian Slavonic Papers 13, nos. 2–3 (1971). Special double issue on
Solzhenitsyn.
  Contains "Point of View Analysis" of *One Day* by Vladimir Rus.

Dunlop, John B., Richard Haugh, and Alexis Klimoff, eds. *Aleksandr
Solzhenitsyn: Critical Essays and Documentary Materials*. 2d ed. New
York: Collier Macmillan, 1975.
  The first edition appeared in 1973, and the second was
  expanded to take into account the publication of *The Gulag
  Archipelago*.
  Of the more than thirty essays in this collection, the one most
  directly bearing on *One Day in the Life of Ivan Denisovich* is
  Terrence Des Pres's "The Heroism of Survival." See also the
  bibliographic surveys by Michael Nicholson on Soviet press
  responses, 1962–73, and by Alexis Klimoff on Solzhenitsyn in
  English.

Dunlop, John B., Richard Haugh, and Michael Nicholson, eds.
Solzhenitsyn in Exile: Critical Essays and Documentary Materials.
Stanford, Calif.: Hoover Institution Press, 1985.
  Includes surveys of the reception of Solzhenitsyn in the United
  States and Europe, and Michael Nicholson's valuable
  "Bibliographical Reorientation" concerning the canon of
  Solzhenitsyn's works.

Ericson, Edward E., Jr. *Solzhenitsyn and the Modern World*.
Washington, D.C.: Regnery Gateway, 1993.
  The most detailed available account of the reception of
  Solzhenitsyn's works and statements in the West, primarily in the
  United States. Ericson points out and rebuts the innumerable
  misapprehensions that have affected the way Solzhenitsyn's message
  has been interpreted.

Feuer, Kathryn, ed. *Solzhenitsyn: A Collection of Critical Essays*.
Englewood Cliffs, N.J.: Prentice-Hall, 1976.
  A well-edited collection of essays, with an excellent
  introduction.

Fiene, Donald. *Alexander Solzhenitsyn: An International Bibliography of Writings by and about Him, 1962–1973*. Ann Arbor, Mich.: Ardis, 1973.

The most complete bibliography for the period indicated. For bibliographical coverage of the subsequent period, see *Solzhenitsyn Studies* (1980–81), the 1985 volume edited by Dunlop, Haugh, and Nicholson, and the compilation by Levitskaia.

Klimoff, Alexis. "Solzhenitsyn in English: An Evaluation." In Dunlop, Haugh, and Klimoff, pp. 611–35.

A cheerless survey, including an examination of the five versions of *One Day* that had appeared by 1971.

———. "Aleksandr Solzhenitsyn." In George Stade, ed., *European Writers: The Twentieth Century*, vol. 13, pp. 3187–3213. New York: Charles Schribner's, 1990.

An overview of Solzhenitsyn's life and works up to 1989.

Korotkov, A. V., S. A. Mel'chin, and S. A. Stepanov, comps. *Kremlevskii samosud: Sekretnye dokumenty Politburo o pisatele A. Solzhenitsyne*. Moscow: Rodina/edition q, 1994.

A collection of reports received and resolutions made by the Soviet leadership in connection with Solzhenitsyn, indicating the regime's obsessive preoccupation with the writer's activities. The period covered is from 1965 to 1980.

Translated as *The Solzhenitsyn Files*, edited by Michael Scammell.

Labedz, Leopold, ed. *Solzhenitsyn: A Documentary Record*. Enlarged ed. Bloomington: Indiana University Press, 1973.

An important sourcebook on the political storms that raged around Solzhenitsyn in the period before his exile.

Lakshin, Vladimir. *Solzhenitsyn, Tvardovsky, and Novy Mir*. Translated by Michael Glenny. Cambridge, Mass.: MIT Press, 1980.

Lakshin responds with some heat to what he considers Solzhenitsyn's unfair portrayal of Tvardovsky and *Novy Mir* in *The Oak and the Calf*. (But in a prefatory note to a new publication of his essay, he expresses regret at the intemperate tone of his earlier statement. See Vladimir Lakshin, *Berega kul'tury* [Moscow: MIROS, 1994], p. 327.)

The MIT edition also contains two substantial essays on Tvardovsky and the fate of *Novy Mir*.

———. "*Novyi mir*" *vo vremena Khrushcheva: Dnevnik i poputnoe (1953–1964)*. Moscow: Knizhnaia palata, 1991.

An invaluable source of information about the inner workings of the Soviet Union's most prestigious literary magazine in the post-Stalin period. The publication of *One Day* is a prominent subject.

Levitskaia, N. G. *Aleksandr Solzhenitsyn. Biobibliograficheskii ukazatel'. Avgust 1988–1990.* Moscow: Sovetskii fond kul'tury, 1991.

A compilation focused on the transitional period between the first open mention of Solzhenitsyn's name in the Soviet press after his exile and the appearance of his works in the major literary journals.

Moody, Christopher. *Solzhenitsyn.* 2d rev. ed. New York: Barnes and Noble, 1975.

A stimulating general introduction, with the second edition produced to take into account *The Gulag Archipelago.* The chapter on *One Day* is excellent.

Nicholson, Michael A. "Aleksandr Solzhenitsyn: A Bibliography of Responses in the Official Soviet Press from November 1962 to April 1973." In Dunlop, Haugh, and Klimoff, *Aleksandr Solzhenitsyn,* pp. 579–610.

This work includes references to all the major published reactions to *One Day.*

———. "Solzhenitsyn as 'Socialist Realist.'" In H. Chung et al., eds., *In the Party Spirit: Socialist Realism and Literary Practice in the Soviet Union, East Germany and China,* pp. 55–68. Amsterdam: Rodopi, 1996.

A definitive analysis of a question that has been raised by some commentators who have tried to link Solzhenitsyn to this doctrine.

Nivat, Georges. *Soljénitsyne.* Paris: Seuil, 1980.

The best introduction to Solzhenitsyn's life and works in any language. No English translation exists, but there is a Russian translation, updated by Nivat: Zhorzh Niva, *Solzhenitsyn,* translated from the French by Simon Markish (London: OPI, 1984). Reprinted in Moscow by the Khudozhestvennaia literatura publishing house in 1992.

Remnick, David. "The Exile Returns." In *The New Yorker* 69, no. 50 (February 14, 1994): 64–83.

A lucidly written essay that attempts to provide an overall evaluation of Solzhenitsyn on the eve of his return to Russia after twenty years in the West. Reprinted, in slightly revised form, as a chapter in Remnick's book *Resurrection: The Struggle for a New Russia.* New York: Random House, 1997.

Scammell, Michael. *Solzhenitsyn: A Biography.* New York: Norton, 1984.

This massive volume contains the fullest available account of Solzhenitsyn's life in the years before he achieved fame. The story of the publication of *One Day* is traced in great detail. Scammell's comments on the literary works are less successful, and his account of events from the mid-1960s on is marked by an overreliance on the memoirs of Solzhenitsyn's first wife.

————, ed. *The Solzhenitsyn Files: Secret Soviet Documents Reveal One Man's Fight against the Monolith*. Translated under the supervision of Catherine A. Fitzpatrick. Chicago: edition q, 1995.

A translation (with numerous mistakes and some omissions) of *Kremlevskii samosud*, edited by Korotkov et al.

Schillinger, John A., guest ed. *Modern Fiction Studies* 23, no. 1 (Spring 1977) (special issue on Aleksandr Solzhenitsyn).

Contains Gary Kern's important "Ivan the Worker."

Shneerson, Mariia. *Aleksandr Solzhenitsyn: Ocherki tvorchestva*. Frankfurt a/M: Posev, 1984.

A useful overview, but one that displays a lack of familiarity with the non-Russian critical literature.

Solzhenitsyn Studies. A Quarterly Survey 1, no. 1 (1980) to 2, no. 1 (1981).

A mine of information, unfortunately discontinued after five issues.

Works Bearing on *One Day in the Life of Ivan Denisovich*

Al'tshuller, Mark, and Elena Dryzhakova. "Tainy Gulaga otkryvaiutsia vsem." In their *Put' otrecheniia: Russkaia literatura 1953–1968*, pp. 158–72. Tenafly, N.J.: Ermitazh, 1985.

An excellent analysis of *One Day*, one that successfully integrates the political and aesthetic aspects of the work.

Anon. "K 25-letiiu vykhoda v svet povesti 'Odin den' Ivana Denisovicha.'" *Vestnik Russkogo Khristianskogo Dvizheniia*, no. 150 (1987): 72–90.

A samizdat collection of early responses in the Soviet provincial press, followed by a detailed analysis of the historical circumstances revealed in and implied by *One Day*.

Chukovskaia, Lidiia. *Zapiski ob Anne Akhmatovoi*. Vol. 2. Paris: YMCA Press, 1980.

Chukovskaia's diary entries record Anna Akhmatov's response to *One Day*. The most important passages are on pages 431, 449, 450, 464, and 469.

Des Pres, Terrence. "The Heroism of Survival." In Dunlop, Haugh, and Klimoff, eds., pp. 45–62.

An eloquent statement of the moral significance of survival in conditions such as those facing Shukhov.

Dunn, John F. *"Ein Tag" vom Standpunkt eines Lebens: Ideelle Konsequenz als Gestaltungsfaktor im erzahlerischen Werk von Aleksandr Isaevich Solzhenitsyn.* Munich: Otto Sagner, 1988.

An ambitious attempt to use the structure, narrative mode, and stylistic devices of *One Day* as a means for approaching other works of Solzhenitsyn, primarily *August 1914.* Written in Germanic dissertation style.

Erlich, Victor. "Post-Stalin Trends in Russian Literature." *Slavic Review* 23, no. 3 (September 1964): 405–19.

A vigorously stated critique of what is seen as a structural weakness of *One Day in the Life of Ivan Denisovich.*

———. "Reply." *Slavic Review* 23, no. 3 (September 1964): 437–40.

Includes a response to Max Hayward's defense of Solzhenitsyn's *One Day.*

Fridlender, G. M. "O Solzhenitsyne i ego estetike." *Russkaia literatura,* 1993, no. 1: 92–99.

Contains useful observations, especially on the phonetic patterns and rhythmic structures of *One Day,* but errs in the presentation of factual data such as the sequence of Solzhenitsyn's works.

Hayward, Max. "Solzhenitsyn's Place in Contemporary Soviet Literature." *Slavic Review* 23, no. 3 (September 1964): 432–36.

Polemical response to Victor Erlich's remarks on Solzhenit- syn.

Kern, Gary. "Solzhenitsyn's Self-Censorship: The Canonical Text of *Odin den' Ivana Denisovicha.*" *Slavic and East European Journal* 20, no. 4 (1976): 421–36.

A meticulous compendium of all textual differences among the Russian-language editions of *One Day* through 1973. Does not consider the *Collected Works* edition, which appeared in 1978.

———. "Ivan the Worker." *Modern Fiction Studies* 23, no. 1 (Spring 1977): 5–30.

Excellent treatment of several aspects of *One Day,* burdened by a lengthy discussion of Marx's theory of alienation (which sheds no useful light on Solzhenitsyn's work).

Lakshin, Vladimir. "Ivan Denisovich, ego druz'ia i nedrugi." *Novyi mir,* 1964, no. 1: 223–45.

A review of the major critical reactions to *One Day* in the Soviet press from a point of view sympathetic to Solzhenitsyn.

Partial translation available in Priscilla Johnson and Leopold Labedz, eds., *Khrushchev and the Arts: The Politics of Soviet Culture, 1962–1964* (Cambridge, Mass.: MIT Press, 1965), pp. 275–88.

Leighton, Lauren G. "On Translation: *One Day in the Life of Ivan Denisovich.*" *Russian Language Journal* 32, no. 111 (1978): 117–30.

A close look at the five English translations of *One Day* produced by 1978. Does not examine the H. T. Willetts translation (published in 1991).

Luplow, Richard. "Narrative Style and Structure in *One Day in the Life of Ivan Denisovich.*" *Russian Literature Triquarterly* 1 (1971): 399–412.

Argues that a distinction must be made between Shukhov's voice and the *skaz*-type account of a generalized narrator. The examples chosen to illustrate this thesis, however, fail to take into account the fact that Solzhenitsyn has included some passages in manifestly nonpeasant style.

Mihajlov, Mihajlo. "Dostoevsky's and Solzhenitsyn's *House of the Dead.*" In his *Russian Themes*, trans. Marija Mihailov, pp. 78–118. New York: Farrar Straus Giroux, 1968.

Useful, though excessively long-winded comparison.

Nekrasov, Viktor. "Isaichu . . . " *Kontinent*, no. 18 (1978): 3–5 (special supplement).

Recollections of the events surrounding the publication of *One Day* in 1962.

Oja, Matt F. "Shalamov, Solzhenitsyn, and the Mission of Memory." *Survey* 29, no. 2 (1985): 62–69.

A stimulating comparison of the views of the two most famous chroniclers of the Soviet Gulag.

Orlova, Raisa. "Chto ia znala o rabakh." In her *Vospominaniia o neproshedshem vremeni*, pp. 215–23. Moscow: Slovo, 1993.

The wife of Lev Kopelev gives her brief but important recollections of the circumstances related to the publication of *One Day*.

Pike, David. "A Camp Through the Eyes of a Peasant: Solzhenitsyn's *One Day in the Life of Ivan Denisovich.*" *California Slavic Studies* 10 (1977): 193–223.

Contains numerous excellent comments on the general structure of *One Day*.

Rus, Vladimir J. "*One Day in the Life of Ivan Denisovich*: A Point of View Analysis." *Canadian Slavonic Papers* 13, nos. 2–3 (1971): 165–78.

A sophisticated, and in an important sense oversophisticated, analysis of the narrative strategies of *One Day*.

Ruttner, Eckhard. "The Names in Solzhenitsyn's Short Novel: *One Day in the Life of Ivan Denisovich*." *Names* 23 (1975): 103–11.

Interesting but not always persuasive attempt to extract meaning from several surnames and given names in *One Day*.

Rzhevskii, Leonid. "Obraz rasskazchika v povesti Solzhenitsyna 'Odin den' Ivana Denisovicha.'" In Robert Magidoff et al., eds., *Studies in Slavic Linguistics and Poetics: In Honor of Boris O. Unbegaun*, pp. 165–78. New York: New York University Press, 1968.

The primary focus is on semantic and phraseological levels of the text. The difficulty of distinguishing the voice of Shukhov from that of a general narrator is noted.

Shalamov, Varlam. Letter to Solzhenitsyn on *One Day*. In *Shalamovskii sbornik*, Vyp. 1, pp. 64–75. Vologda: Izdanie instituta povysheniia kvalifikatsii pedagogicheskikh kadrov, 1994.

An enthusiastic evaluation of *One Day* alternates with commentary on ways the camp Solzhenitsyn depicted differs from the camp Shalamov experienced.

Shneerson, Mariia. "Golos Shukhova v proizvedeniiakh Solzhenitsyna." *Grani*, no. 146 (1987): 106–33.

An attempt to show that Shukhov's somewhat skeptical tone of voice can be identified in a number of Solzhenitsyn's later works such as *The Gulag Archipelago* and *The Oak and the Calf*.

Solzhenitsyn, Aleksandr. "How People Read *One Day*." In Leopold Labedz, ed., *Solzhenitsyn: A Documentary Record*, enlarged ed., pp. 44–62. Bloomington: Indiana University Press, 1973.

A survey of letters received from readers of *One Day*.

———. "Interv'iu dlia radio Bi-Bi-Si." *Vestnik Russkogo Khristianskogo Dvizheniia*, no. 138 (1983): 155–63.

Interview by Barry Holland of the BBC's Russian Service on the occasion of the twentieth anniversary of the publication of *One Day*. Contains important comments by the author not available elsewhere.

Thompson, Margareta O. "Tvardovskii's Unpublished Letters to Makedonov." *Russian Language Journal* 48, nos. 159–61 (1994): 193–212.

Several letters touch on Solzhenitsyn's *One Day*, and all are useful for characterizing Tvardovsky.

Toker, L. "On Some Aspects of the Narrative Method in *One Day in the Life of Ivan Denisovich*." In W. Moskovich, ed., *Russian Philology and History: In Honor of Professor Victor Levin*, pp. 270–82. Jerusalem: Hebrew University, 1992.
Contains numerous acute observations.

Vinokur, T. G. "O iazyke i stile povesti A. I. Solzhenitsyna 'Odin den' Ivana Denisovicha.'" *Voprosy kul'tury rechi*, 1965, no. 6: 16–32.
A seminal analysis of the stylistic features of *One Day*.

Miscellaneous

A. Solzhenitsyn chitaet "Odin den'Ivana Denisovicha." BBC production. London, 1983.
Tape recording of Solzhenitsyn reading of the full text of *One Day*. Available in the U.S. in a three-cassette format from Audio Forum of Guilford, Conn.

Wrede, Casper, director. *One Day in the Life of Ivan Denisovich*. Produced by Group W-Leontief-Norskfilm, 1971.
The film is closely based on Solzhenitsyn's text, and features Tom Courtenay in the title role.

Contributors

Robert Louis Jackson is B. E. Bensinger Professor of Slavic Languages and Literatures at Yale University. Besides his articles on Pushkin, Gogol, Chekhov, Tolstoy, Turgenev, Tiutchev, V. I. Ivanov, and other Russian writers, he is the author of *Dialogues with Dostoevsky: The Overwhelming Questions* (1993) and three other books on Dostoevsky as well as several collections of essays on Chekhov and Dostoevsky.

Alexis Klimoff, editor of this volume, is Professor of Russian at Vassar College. He has coedited a book of essays on Solzhenitsyn and is the author of articles on nineteenth- and twentieth-century Russian literature. He has also translated a number of Solzhenitsyn's works.

Richard Tempest is Associate Professor of Slavic Languages and Literatures at the University of Illinois at Urbana-Champaign. He is the coeditor of Pierre Tchaadaev, *Oeuvres inédites ou rares* (Paris, 1990) and *The Philosophical Works of Peter Chaadaev* (Dordrecht-Boston-London, 1991) and is the author of numerous articles on nineteenth- and twentieth-century Russian literature and Russian intellectual history.

Dariusz Tolczyk is Assistant Professor of Slavic Languages and Literatures at the University of Virginia. His main interest is Russian and Polish literature, especially relationships between literature and ideology. He is the author of *See No Evil: Literary Cover-Ups and Discoveries of the Soviet Camp Experience* (New Haven, Conn.: Yale University Press, forthcoming), and articles in *Partisan Review*, *The Polish Review*, and other American and Polish journals and collections.